THREE PLAYS

Also by John Ashbery

POETRY

Turandot and Other Poems
Some Trees
The Tennis Court Oath
Rivers and Mountains
Selected Poems
The Double Dream of Spring
Three Poems
Self-Portrait in a Convex Mirror
Houseboat Days
As We Know
Shadow Train

FICTION
with James Schuyler

A Nest of Ninnies

THREE PLAYS
by
John Ashbery

WITHDRAWN

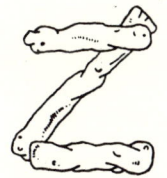

Z PRESS

CALAIS · VERMONT

1982

Caution: Professionals and amateurs are hereby warned that these plays, being fully protected under the Universal Copyright Convention, are subject to royalty. All rights, including professional, amateur, motion picture, recitation, public reading, radio and television broadcasting, and the rights of translation into foreign languages, are strictly reserved. Inquiries should be directed to John Ashbery, c/o Georges Borchardt, Inc., 145 East 52nd Street, New York, New York 10022, U.S.A.

Acknowledgment is made to the following publications in which these plays first appeared: "The Heroes": *Artists' Theatre*, edited by Herbert Machiz (Grove Press, 1960); "The Compromise": *The Hasty Papers*, edited and published by Alfred Leslie (1960); "The Philosopher": *Art and Literature*, 2 (1964).

The publication of this book was made possible by a grant from the National Endowment for the Arts in Washington D.C., a Federal Agency.

Front cover by Joe Brainard

Z Press Publications are edited by
KENWARD ELMSLIE

Second Edition, printed by the
Northlight Studio Press, Barre, Vermont

Designed and printed in Lunenburg, Vermont,
in November 1977 by The Stinehour Press.
This edition is limited to 1000 copies in
paper wrappers, 500 numbered hardcover
copies, and 26 lettered and signed
hardcover copies.

COPYRIGHT © 1960, 1961, 1964, 1978 BY JOHN ASHBERY
ALL RIGHTS RESERVED
LIBRARY OF CONGRESS CATALOG NUMBER 77-92578
HARDCOVER: ISBN 0-915990-12-1
PAPER: ISBN 0-915990-13-X

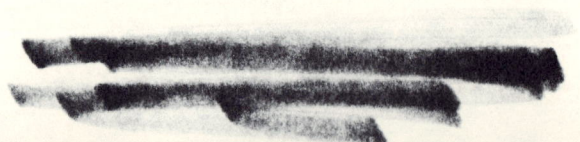

Contents

THE HEROES   1

THE COMPROMISE   31

THE PHILOSOPHER   121

THE HEROES

CHARACTERS

Achilles
Circe
Ulysses
Hebe
Patroclus
Chorus
Astyanax
Theseus
Guard
Andromache
Hector

Place: A country house near the sea.

Scene: A living room of an undeterminable period. Theseus and Patroclus are sitting around in costumes that are vaguely Greek.

THESEUS

... I took advantage of the fact that it was built like a maze. Whenever you do this, even if the problem is just one in algebra, everything becomes simple immediately. Because then you can sit back and get a picture of yourself doing whatever it is. If you do not grant its own peculiar nature to the problem, you can have no picture of yourself and consequently feel harassed and lonely. Without imagination nothing can be easy.

PATROCLUS

How wonderful everything sounds when you tell about it.

THESEUS
(*He seems confused.*)

No ... that's not right. Say—do you think I could have a drink?

PATROCLUS
(*smiling*)

Oh certainly. (*He rings.*) You must forgive me for my laxity.... But do go on with your story. I can't tell you how interesting it sounds to one who has spent the best years of his life pent up in this great old stupid house.

THESEUS

It must be rather dull for you here, Patroclus.

PATROCLUS

Dull! I have to get up early every day because that brute won't allow breakfast to be served at any other time. Then I'm left to myself all day, poking around the stables or going for walks—or *a* walk, rather, because there's only one.

THESEUS

But I should think Achilles would be an agreeable companion.

PATROCLUS

Oh, I hardly ever see him except at cocktails, and sometimes we go for a swim after dinner. He's pleasant enough. But I'm starved for intellectual conversation. We don't get the books or magazines till they've been out a month.

THESEUS

Does Achilles read much?

PATROCLUS

Oh forget about him. Talk some more about the minotaur.

THESEUS

I've never told anyone about it before.

PATROCLUS

Oh. . . . But I promise it will be a secret.

THESEUS

You're very sweet. Well, as I think I said, the minotaur itself was the least important part of the whole scheme. I'd always supposed the world was full of fakes, but I was foolish enough to believe that it was made interesting by the varying degrees of skill with which they covered up their lack of integrity. It never occurred to me that the greatest fake of all would make not the slightest effort to convince me of its reality . . . not a pretense! But there it was—a stupid, unambitious piece of stage machinery.

THE HEROES

PATROCLUS

Incredible! But perhaps that was exactly Daedalus' intention.

THESEUS

What?

PATROCLUS

To take you off your guard that way.

THESEUS

But to what purpose? There was nothing to do but give the thing a well-aimed kick and go home.

PATROCLUS

But what about all the maidens it was supposed to have devoured?

THESEUS

All dead.
(*Hebe enters.*)

HEBE

Yes, sir.

PATROCLUS

Two drinks please. And oh, Hebe, would you tell Achilles our guest has arrived.

HEBE

He's gone hunting, sir.

PATROCLUS

Oh. . . . Isn't that just like him!
(*Patroclus has been staring at Theseus.*)

THESEUS

Look here, Patroclus, would you really care to know what it was like?

PATROCLUS

Oh yes!

THESEUS

Very well. You must use your imagination. Hebe, you stand here and be Ariadne. You must hold the end of this ball of yarn and on no account let go. Patroclus, you get on the landing and pretend to be the monster. This is the picture: the door to the labyrinth is like the entrance to a vast fun-house in some deserted amusement park. The structure is built of old planks and extends as far as the eye can see. Part of it sprawls up the hillside like a fantastic vineyard; another part has been slowly sinking into a salt-marsh a mile or so away. The weather is oppressive. Behind Ariadne and me the sea is making a small but terrible noise.

PATROCLUS
(beginning to be excited)

You make everything sound so wonderful!

THESEUS

Now we are inside. Nothing but endless vistas. Old posters peeling off the walls, a smell of urine, the wind sighing through the cracks in the planks. We descend five little steps, turn a corner, and walk up five more steps. This stupid device is one of Daedalus' favorite bedevilments. Sometimes the cracks in the planks admit sand. There are frequent large holes in the roof, so the visitor is free, if he wishes, to climb out on top and survey the ground plan of the whole edifice. In short, he is in the dubious position of a person who believes that dada is still alive.
(Patroclus and Hebe are showing signs of intense excitement.)
Now comes the strangest part of all. You have been in the maze several days and nights, and you are beginning to realize that you have changed several times. Not just you, either, but your whole idea of the maze and the maze itself. This is most difficult to explain, and it is the wickedest thing Daedalus ever did. The maze looks just about the same as ever—it is more as if it were being looked at by a different person.

HEBE
(recklessly)

I understand!
(*It has grown darker. Theseus has been winding his way through the furniture toward Patroclus.*)

THESEUS

The horror and fascination with which I navigated that last wooden passage! How dark it was! A waterfall is sounding all around me. It is inside my head. But I was so happy—happy, Patroclus! For now at last I was seeing myself as I could only be—not as I might be seen by a person in the street: full of unfamiliarity and the resulting poetry. Before, I might have seemed beautiful to the passerby. I now seemed ten times more so to myself, for I saw that I meant nothing beyond the equivocal statement of my limbs and the space and time they happened to occupy.

PATROCLUS
(full of love)

Go on!

THESEUS

I realized that I now possessed the only weapon with which the minotaur might be vanquished—the indifference of a true aesthete. Drawing my sword with as much assurance as you might deal a card, I kicked open the door to the little privy-like enclosure where he lay. There was nothing there but a great big doodle-bug made of wood and painted canvas.

PATROCLUS
(hysterically)

But what about the maidens! You said they were all dead!
(*Theseus rushes forward and grasps Patroclus about the middle, lifting him above his head. Patroclus is sobbing. Hebe faints but recovers immediately.*)

THESEUS

O felicity!
(*The lights go up as Achilles, Circe, and the Chorus enter by the center door. Achilles is just what one expects. Circe looks like Theda Bara and has a slight accent. The Chorus is a stout middle-aged woman in navy-blue robes.*)

ACHILLES and CIRCE

Well!
(*Patroclus crosses to them.*)

PATROCLUS
(*embarrassed*)

Achilles, where have you been? Theseus has been here hours and has been most amusing about his experiences in the labyrinth. Circe, have you two met?

CIRCE

I think we have.

ACHILLES

Theseus—this *is* nice. Make yourself comfortable. Why are you fidgeting so, Patroclus. You seem to want to apologize for something.

PATROCLUS

Oh shut up. You always try to make me feel inferior right at the beginning.

ACHILLES

It's not that, but I know when you've got something on your mind I'll have to hear about it sooner or later.

PATROCLUS

Oh rats.
(*He goes out.*)

ACHILLES

Excuse him all of you. He gets that way. (*slily*) I expect he was jealous, Theseus, when he heard about your exploits.

THESEUS

I'm flattered you think so. I was just giving Patroclus and Hebe here a little blow-by-blow description. (*Achilles glares at Hebe, who goes out.*) I guess we may have gotten a little carried away.

ACHILLES

(*frigidly*)

You may do whatever you like in this house, Theseus. But please, everybody, don't let's stand around like this. Wouldn't you all like to play something? I'm no good as a host.

CIRCE

Excuse please, but aren't you expecting still another guest?

ACHILLES

By George, so we are! And that reminds me I've got to tell Patroclus something.
(*He goes out, with the Chorus.*)

THESEUS

Well, and how have you been, Medea?

CIRCE

The name is Circe! (*Theseus has already turned to blush for his mistake.*) It's all right. I know what witchcraft does to a woman's face.

THESEUS

Forgive me. You're a very beautiful woman.

CIRCE

Oh that we have to converse in this way! Why can't each one say just what he thinks? If you men would only have the nerve to say, "Circe, you're a disgusting old bag!" Then after we got the insults out of the way we might accomplish something. Stop calling each other dearie. This way we no more resemble human beings than those silly figures on the front of the Parthenon do.

THESEUS

Excuse me, Circe, but I don't agree with you there. I think those figures are beautiful. And I think that people are beautiful in the same way.

CIRCE

I don't get it.

THESEUS

Let me tell you of an experience I had while I was on my way here. My train had stopped in the station directly opposite another. Through the glass I was able to watch a couple in the next train, a man and a woman who were having some sort of conversation. For fifteen minutes I watched them. I had no idea what their relation was. I could form no idea of their conversation. They might have been speaking words of love, or planning a murder, or quarreling about their in-laws. Yet just from watching them talk, even though I could hear nothing, I feel I know those people better than anyone in the world.

CIRCE

You're a strange man.

THESEUS

Coming from you, that must be a compliment.

CIRCE

Kiss me.

THESEUS

Really—

CIRCE

Then don't. I don't know why men always seem to fear me.

THESEUS
(angrily)

Oh how can you. You show me that you weren't even listening to what I just said. You don't even believe what you just told me. I think it

would be best if we spoke as little as possible during the rest of this weekend.
(*He goes out.*)

CIRCE

It's true! They all think they can outsmart me just because I'm a witch! (*She flops down on an ottoman, crying a little.*) Oh I could kill that man! But what if I did? Everybody'd say they always expected it of me! (*She sobs awhile.*) There's only one thing to do. Luckily I brought along this girdle, which will make every man who sees me in it fall hopelessly in love with me. (*She slips it on.*) There we are. Love conquers all, as the poet said.
(*Achilles enters, followed by Patroclus, Theseus, the Chorus, and Ulysses. The last named is very shy. He is wearing tweeds.*)

ACHILLES

Circe! See who's here.
(*Ulysses comes forward and kisses Circe's hand.*)

ULYSSES

Delighted, I'm sure.

CIRCE

You dear thing. I'd almost forgotten you, Ulysses.
(*Ulysses blushes.*)

ACHILLES

Oh by the way, everybody, this is the Chorus.
(*The Chorus bows. They bow.*)

CHORUS

I've been invited to see what's to be done.

THESEUS

What?

CHORUS

Yes, I feel rather like the man from Scotland Yard.

ACHILLES
(*hastily*)
Well, what would anybody like to do? How about a swim before tea?
(*Astyanax enters. He is a boy of about ten.*)

ASTYANAX
Tea is served on the lawn, lords and ladies.
(*They go out chatting, except for Circe and Ulysses, who remain.*)

ULYSSES
It's so strange—our meeting again. So many conversations are forgotten, faces blotted out.

CIRCE
What is there left to say.

ULYSSES
That's the strangest time. When there's nothing. When two ancient personages meet. Known to everybody in the world, disfigured by trash of folklore, excrement of centuries. Two gigantic piles of rubbish, poking through the twilight of the world. And unlike mountains, we're not even thoughtful.

CIRCE
Don't. I've still my life to lead.

ULYSSES
That's what you think.

CIRCE
Don't be so pessimistic, dear. It's true we're famous but that doesn't mean we don't have a private life.

ULYSSES
The only thing we know about each other is that we happen to be in this room.

CIRCE
It's spring. A time for coming together.

ULYSSES
Perhaps. But perhaps not for you and me.
(*They wander off absently through different doors. The Chorus comes in as if to look for them.*)

CHORUS
I have seen many many people in every possible relation to each other and I have never seen any good come of it.
(*A day passes. This is shown by lowering the lights for a few moments and then raising them. The Chorus stands in the same place.*)
So far this play has been easy. From now on it's going to be more difficult to follow. That's the way life is sometimes.
(*Soft music is heard. Circe and Achilles, Theseus and Patroclus, enter at opposite doors and slowly cross the stage, leaving by opposite doors.*)
Yea, a fine stifling mist springs up from the author's pure and moody mind. Confusion and hopelessness follow on the precise speech of spring. Just as, when the last line of this play is uttered, your memory will lift a torch to the dry twisted mass. Then it will not seem so much as if all this never happened, but as if parts continued to go on all the time in your head, rising up without warning whenever you start to do the simplest act. (*Ulysses appears in the doorway at the center.*) Come forth, Ulysses. Why are you here?

ULYSSES
I have nothing to ask for.

CHORUS
What, not even Circe, an earth-born goddess divine?

ULYSSES
I have seen too many places. Too many children know my story.
(*The Chorus seems bored. She strolls over to a window.*)

Ai, regret that will fall on the house of Achilles. Foolish he was to invite Theseus, slayer of monsters. A shadow falls over the hero just before he commits a heroic act.

Just the same, it is the hero alone who can judge the act because of his superior powers. So it must be the audience who is wrong. But since they are all in agreement... !

Achilles, couldn't you have foreseen this difficulty? A hero yourself, greater than any of us.

Why have you let him put conflict between yourself and Patroclus, between Circe and me? Wherever that one goes, he is with others as statues on the face of a building.

Oh Achilles! Theseus! Figures suggesting combat remorse return. Under all, the antique charade.

It is the querulously blue Mediterranean that draws these tears from this old slept-on face. Oh it does not matter who we are!

But there is one thing Theseus does not know. (*The Chorus sighs, and turns to look at Ulysses.*) Every person must be either alive or dead.

CHORUS

Ulysses, I have pretended not to hear, but I was actually listening to every word you said. However, I promise not to reveal it to any of the others.

(*The Chorus and Ulysses shake hands.*)

ULYSSES

We are bound together in an eternal oath.

(*The Chorus goes out. Ulysses goes to the window where she was and looks out. Achilles and Patroclus come on, unaware of him.*)

PATROCLUS

The little schemer!

ACHILLES

Stop criticizing Theseus, Patroclus. You know he influenced you a great deal.

PATROCLUS
I was crying when he lifted me over his head because I thought he would slay me, as he did the minotaur.

ACHILLES
You're lying. He must have told you previously that the minotaur was not a live being.

PATROCLUS
He did. But you know that it was supposed to have devoured a number of youths and maidens. And Theseus said they all perished.

ACHILLES
Were their remains lying near the minotaur?

PATROCLUS
He didn't say.

ACHILLES
There is always a logical explanation for things.

PATROCLUS
(*pensively*)
Either the minotaur was alive or those maidens weren't dead.

ACHILLES
Forget about Theseus. Listen, Patroclus, you know the old story of Circe and Ulysses?

PATROCLUS
The one in the *Odyssey*? Yes.

ACHILLES
I know that Circe hasn't forgotten the affection she had for him once. She wants to get her hooks into him again. And that could cause trouble. A person of her mental make-up might decide to change us all into pigs for no reason at all.

PATROCLUS

I think that would be delicious.

ACHILLES

Stop clowning. You know how funny people get after they've been down here awhile.

PATROCLUS

But the place has no atmosphere whatever!

ACHILLES

Remind Ulysses of his duties to Penelope. Get him out of here. If necessary, make up a phoney telegram.

PATROCLUS

You do it. I can't say any of this interests me in the slightest.
(*He goes out. Achilles turns and discovers Ulysses.*)

ACHILLES

My dear! I had no idea you were here!

ULYSSES

It's all right, Achilles. I'm not interested in Circe. I doubt if she'd try any witchcraft.

ACHILLES

I guess I'm a big coward, really. I wish she'd go. But I don't want to offend her.

ULYSSES

You must act the part of the host. Try organizing us, so each person has something to occupy him.

ACHILLES

That's an idea. We might play some games. After dinner we might have a dance. We could go for a hike. Theseus, Patroclus, and Circe could

take the path around the lake and you and I could take a secret walk I've never shown to anyone before. What on earth!
(*Theseus and Circe come on arm in arm. Ulysses and Achilles hide behind a screen.*)

CIRCE

Light melts along the pillars and pediments of ancient Greece.

THESEUS

O passing cloud.

CIRCE

It's spring. A time for rotting. From pools and cisterns, sewers and manure piles, a fine mist rises to cleanse and later befog the sky-blue lenses of the heart.

THESEUS

O little teaser.

CIRCE

A time for rotting and coming together. Yes, there will soon be no more room for the thoughts we are thinking at this present moment.

THESEUS

Yes. O Circe, I hear a waterfall nearby.

CIRCE

It's too hot to breathe in this stinking fen. What shall we do about it.

THESEUS

We could take off our clothes.
(*Circe begins to disrobe.*)

CIRCE

O the harm. We get too close, and our thoughts get mingled like mud that is trampled underfoot. Then something happens. Another thing happens which makes us forget the first thing, and then generally we are in a different place.

THESEUS

Yes, we are constantly changing, even when we are most aware of it. I'm beginning to think it doesn't mean a thing.

CIRCE

As I was saying, it's that we're always being met, but it seems that we're going out of our way. Even to survey this from a great distance is to be unable to draw a conclusion, for someone again draws close to interrupt, and whispers so that we may not conclude.

THESEUS

It's scurvy. Let me help.

CIRCE

You don't want to help. I don't want you to. There is music though and some peace in the waterfall.

THESEUS

Let's forget everything in a kiss.
(*The girdle falls to the floor. There is sudden darkness, and thunder and lightning outside. Achilles rushes forward dragging Ulysses.*)

ACHILLES

What's this! Come on, everyone, let's go for a walk! A breath of fresh air!
(*He runs off, dragging Ulysses and Circe.*)

ULYSSES
(*as they go off*)

Farewell, Theseus!

THESEUS

Left behind. That's the way it was. She came in, dressed in cold colors. 'Twas an afternoon like this. A smile passed from customer to customer.
(*Theseus falls to his knees, then to the floor, unconscious. The Chorus enters.*)

THE HEROES 19

                    CHORUS
Now we have The Dream of Theseus.
(She goes out. The stage gets very dark. By the light of a setting sun one can now distinguish the plains of Troy. At the left are the gates of the city. A guard is stationed there. At the rear is the sea, bordered by cattails. Martial music is playing. Patroclus enters from the right.)

                    GUARD
Who's there?

                    PATROCLUS
Patroclus.

                    GUARD
What's the password?

                    PATROCLUS
The Cherry Orchard.

                    GUARD
You're taking advantage of the fact that this play is laid in ancient times.

                    PATROCLUS
What better meter?

                    GUARD
Pass in. *(Patroclus exits through the gates. Hebe enters from the right.)* Who's there?

                    HEBE
Nay, stand and unfold yourself.

                    GUARD
The password, then.

                    HEBE
I forgot it.

GUARD

You're trading on your youth, my dear little chick.

HEBE

What sweeter raisin?

GUARD

Pass in. (*Hebe goes off. Astyanax enters.*) Who goes there?

ASTYANAX

The boy Astyanax.

GUARD

I suppose all your little playfellows have gone inside the gates and you'd like to, too.

ASTYANAX

That's about it.

GUARD
(*brutally*)

Well you can't, see. You're too little. Come 'ere. Give us a hug.

ASTYANAX

Who are you, anyway?

GUARD

Don't you recognize me?

ASTYANAX

No.

GUARD

Well come back in half an hour and I'll tell you.
(*Astyanax wanders off upstage playing with a yo-yo. Theseus enters, astride the Trojan horse.*)
Who goes *there*?

THE HEROES

THESEUS

A famous hero, Theseus by name.

GUARD

Is that so. (*He shines a lantern in Theseus' face.*) Oh. I know you. There was a lady here asking for you not half an hour ago.

THESEUS

Well, are you going to let me in?

GUARD

No yer can't. At least not on that thing.

THESEUS

Well, couldn't I leave it outside?

GUARD
(*examining horse*)

Hmm. What do you call this?

THESEUS

It's a monster which I've just slain.

GUARD

Monster! But it's just a big wooden dummy.

THESEUS
(*brightly*)

I know!

GUARD

Well. I oughtn't to but I guess you can go in. But you'll have to come back and collect this thing in half an hour's time, you hear?

THESEUS

Thanks.
(*He hops off the horse and enters Troy. Circe enters looking for the girdle.*)

CIRCE

I know I left it here somewhere.
(*She too passes inside the gates of Troy. Hector and Andromache appear at the upper right of the stage. During this scene the guard draws the horse in through the gates as unobtrusively as possible.*)

ANDROMACHE

It's a blessed relief to get out of that hot city for a breath of fresh air, even if it's only for a minute.

HECTOR

Yes, but keep in mind my dear that we're doing it for a purpose.

ANDROMACHE

You mean we've got to keep our eyes open for Grecian scouts.

HECTOR

No, it's not that. We must give those inside a chance to talk about us. I hate it when I know people are thinking things about me. Only after everything has been said can peace come and a good night's rest.

ANDROMACHE

Tee hee. I love the moonlight on the waters.

HECTOR

I often think I'm completely destitute of imagination.
(*Hector and Andromache stand facing Astyanax at a distance, their arms outstretched.*)

ASTYANAX

Father! Mother!

HECTOR

Our boy!
(*An immense explosion inside the walls of Troy fills the sky with light. There is almost complete darkness at once. The Chorus runs on stage, pretending to be Cassandra.*)

THE HEROES 23

CHORUS

It's happened and I'm glad! I told Priam that a beautiful woman would bring us harm. But they thought I was jealous of her and Paris. I tell you once more, men of earth, whatever I say, goes. O glad gift of prophecy! O tongue of conviction! But Theseus has wrought this damage, and he must suffer for it. Where is that man. Lightly he strode into Troy, but appalling will be his exit. And never shall he subdue the monster he has become. Let me out of here.

(*She runs off. The lights come on. The scene is again the living room of Achilles. A phonograph is playing dance music. At the center is a table with a glass and a bottle from which Ulysses frequently helps himself. The following are dancing together: Hebe and Patroclus, Chorus and Theseus, Circe and Achilles. There is general conversation.*)

PATROCLUS

You dance divinely, Hebe.

HEBE

I learned how before I could walk.

ASTYANAX

May I cut in.

HEBE
(*in a stage-whisper*)

Oh save me from that fiendish brat!
(*Astyanax shrugs and walks away.*)

CHORUS

May I ask you a question?

THESEUS

Do.

CHORUS

Weren't you awfully scared in the labyrinth?

THESEUS
Not really. I felt it was quite natural that I should be there.

CHORUS
But didn't the minotaur frighten you?

THESEUS
No. You see, he wasn't alive, really.

CHORUS
But he's supposed to have killed a lot of people.

THESEUS
That's something that's always puzzled me.

CHORUS
Did you see any signs of them in the labyrinth?

THESEUS
Well, I was so keyed up that I didn't notice.

CHORUS
Then how do you know they're dead?

THESEUS
I just have a feeling.

CIRCE
I certainly love your place here, Achilles.

ACHILLES
Yes, we like it.

CIRCE
I think you're the real hero of this occasion. Providing all these activities for us so we don't become bored or sleepy.

ACHILLES
Oh! But it was Ulysses' idea that we have this little dance.

CIRCE

He's so clever.

ACHILLES
(slily)

No doubt you and he have found lots to talk over.

CIRCE

Yes, he's been most attentive.

ULYSSES
(taking a drink)

I heard that remark, Circe, and I'll tell you it's all because of that girdle you've been wearing.
(Everyone laughs.)

ACHILLES

I see you're not wearing it any more.

CIRCE

Oh, I gave it to Theseus. He's been going around saying everybody hates him.

ACHILLES

What about you and him?

CIRCE

Oh, that! It was all because I tried on my magic girdle and he saw me in it. Those things never last.

ACHILLES

I may as well tell you, dear, that everybody has known all about that girdle for years. Theseus did too because I heard him mention it.

CIRCE

Really! Then do you suppose he was serious when he . . .

ASTYANAX

May I cut in.
(*He does so. Achilles dances with the Chorus, Ulysses with Hebe.*)

PATROCLUS

Won't you dance with me, Theseus? (*They dance.*) Sometimes I feel so romantic. As if I were up there, circling with the planets in the night wind. I hear forest murmurs. But then Achilles comes back. If only he'd either pay some attention to me or leave me alone entirely, one or the other.

THESEUS

There, don't cry.

PATROCLUS

It's terrible, Theseus. But I feel better since you got here. Why don't you make your home with us for a little while?

THESEUS

I've got to get on. I sometimes feel as if I'm still in the maze, and that to stop anywhere would be as pointless as to continue.

PATROCLUS

Oh Theseus, mayn't I sleep at the foot of your bed tonight, like a pet spaniel? I promise I'll lie still as a mummy.

THESEUS

Ackgh! You're revolting!
(*He breaks away from Patroclus and goes out.*)

PATROCLUS

Oh, dear! I must have said something to hurt him!
(*He falls on the couch, sobbing. The guard enters dressed as a policeman.*)

GUARD

A nice friendly little gathering, what?

ACHILLES

Stop! No doubt you've been ordered to slay us all at once and ask questions afterward.

GUARD

No. I just want to ask some questions.

CIRCE

Sir, are you aware this is a private dwelling? Have you a warrant?

GUARD

Well no, lady, I haven't. Say, didn't I see you somewhere recently? (*Circe turns her back.*) Sure, I remember. It was outside the walls of Troy. Kinda funny place to be, wasn't it?

CIRCE

I was looking for an article of clothing which I'd dropped.

GUARD
(*politely*)

I see. Would you mind producing it, please? We need evidence.

ULYSSES
(*drunk*)

You always need evidence. But you aren't going to find any, so there.

CIRCE

I gave it to a gentleman who's out of the room at present.

GUARD

I see. And this is the corpse? (*He goes over to Patroclus and feels his pulse.*) As I thought. All right. Who did it?
(*There is a horrified silence. Achilles rushes to the couch and lifts Patroclus.*)

ACHILLES
(*weeping*)

My poor baby! So they got you at last. I curse all the gods for this, miserable unbiased magicians. How could they? Come, Skippy. *Ton papa* is going to take you up that nice walk he never told you about. (*He goes off, bearing the body of Patroclus.*)

GUARD
(*to Astyanax*)

Now button up your coat, my little man. You and I are going for a walk too.
(*Astyanax screams.*)

CHORUS

Don't touch that child, you vile thing. He knows nothing of the crime. Patroclus died of a broken heart.

GUARD

What trashy evidence.

ULYSSES

Will no one mystify me?
(*Theseus returns with a suitcase.*)

THESEUS

Where's Achilles?

CHORUS

He's gone out, probably to do away with himself.

THESEUS

Then you'll say goodbye to him for me. I'm getting out of here.

ULYSSES

Isn't it enough that you've wrecked all our lives, or at least made them unrecognizable? Are you going to leave us here with what we've saved you from?

THESEUS

I've never had such a terrible time! I can't even remember what my life was like before I came here. (*To the Guard*) Why don't you arrest me and take me to prison?

GUARD
(*darkly*)

No. thanks. We've had enough of you.

THESEUS

I don't know why everyone always picks on me!
(*He goes off.*)

ULYSSES

I always thought he knew!

CURTAIN

THE COMPROMISE

CHARACTERS

Captain Harry Reynolds, of the
   Canadian Mounted Police
Margaret Reynolds, his wife
Jim Reynolds, their son
Lieutenant Allan Dale,
   also of the Mounties
Sam Dexter, manager of the
   Cariboo trading post
Lucky Seven, his Indian henchman
Mooka, the Reynolds' Indian maidservant
Chief of the Tobi Indians
Running Deer ⎫
Mountain Lion ⎭ his sons
Daisy Farrell, an entertainer
Blue Feather, an Indian
An Indian sentry
A squaw
The author of the play
A raven
Chorus of Indians

The first two acts take place in the year 1920; the third in 1925. The setting for all three acts is the Canadian North Woods.

ACT I

The interior of a cabin in the North Woods. Margaret is rocking the cradle of her young son, Jim. A fire is burning on the hearth, near which sits Mooka, who chews disgruntledly on a corn-cob pipe.

MARGARET

How like his father he is, Mooka. When he yawns and rubs his eyes like that I could almost imagine it was Harry doing it.

MOOKA

Ugh!

MARGARET
(to the baby)

You certainly do take after him. You've got his same blue eyes and brown, curly hair.

MOOKA

Ugh!

MARGARET

And what's more, you've got his cheerful disposition. I know you're going to be a good, brave, honest, cheerful man just like your dad.

MOOKA

Ugh!

MARGARET

Mooka, I won't have you talking that way about Harry. He's a fine man and my husband, so let's not hear any more about it. Moreover this is his house and not yours.

MOOKA

Him leave white missus. Him no good.

MARGARET

That's not true! You know the Mounties are often gone months and even years on a mission. "They always get their man." And Harry's not been gone a year yet.
(*She glances at the calendar.*)

MOOKA

White missus know him gone longer—exactly one year and three days!

MARGARET
(*dabbing at her eyes with a handkerchief*)

Oh . . . is it?

MOOKA

White missus a fool! White master no gone after criminal.

MARGARET

Why, what do you mean?

MOOKA

Mooka's boy friend, Lucky Seven, him say him see Captain Harry in Elk City, in saloon. Him tell dancing girl him not married. Then Lucky Seven say him follow dancing girl into dressing room.

MARGARET

That's a lie! You get out of here, you lying old witch!

THE COMPROMISE 35

MOOKA

(*comes over and kneels before Margaret*)

Mooka want only white missus' happiness! Mooka at first not want to tell, me swear!

If only missus would gettum divorce. Then maybe Dexter, manager of trading post, propose to her. Him sweet on white missus already. Mooka watch, Mooka see how him look at her whenever her go in store. Dexter rich man, powerful man. Him maybe build us fine house here in Cariboo, or move away altogether. North Woods no fit place to bringum up son. Him makum fine father to little Jim, white missus see.

Captain Harry, him maybe not bad man at heart, but him no good husband! Him no bring up son in right way. Dexter, him make good husband and father.

MARGARET

(*She has shown signs of wavering, but finally becomes resolute again.*)
That will do, Mooka. I know you mean well with your advice, but you seem to forget that I have certain responsibilities toward my husband. Even if I cared for Mr. Dexter, which I don't, I gave a promise to Harry to wait for him . . . though he has been gone an awfully long time!

MOOKA

Him gone . . . too long!

MARGARET

Mooka, why don't you wash up those dishes in the kitchen while I tidy up in here a bit? A little housework might revive our spirits.

MOOKA
(*glumly*)

Yes, missus.
(*She bows and goes off to the left.*)

MARGARET

(*gazing fondly into the cradle*)

Poor little fellow! Supposing what they say about your father is true? (*looking at the audience*) He must never know!
(*A knock is heard at the door; Margaret expresses the emotions of fear, hope, and joy before rushing to open it. Just as she gets to the door it bursts open and Lucky Seven, a villainous-looking Indian, lunges into the room.*)
Eeek! Oh, it's you, Lucky Seven. Goodness, can't you come into a room like ordinary people? (*She sees others.*) And Mr. Dexter! And Allan! But ... who are these other men?
(*Dexter, Dale, Chief, and Chorus of Indians enter.*)

DEXTER

Perhaps you'd like to explain that, Lieutenant Dale.

DALE

Margaret ...

MARGARET

Well, what is it? Why are you all looking at me that way?

DALE

I'm afraid what I have to say may come as a shock ...

MARGARET

Allan dear, won't you ever learn not to beat around the bush? Out with it, man!

DALE

Very well. This man (*pointing to the Chief, who bows*) is the Chief of the Tobi Indians, who have the big settlement near Elk City.

MARGARET

Elk City!

DALE

Yes. Why have you turned pale?

MARGARET
It's nothing. Go on with what you were saying.

DALE
The chief brings disturbing news from his settlement. It seems that a desperado has been robbing the Indians in the area, coming into their homes at night, threatening them, even molesting their wives. In short he has terrorized the whole neighborhood. This man . . . This man is . . . I can't go on!

DEXTER
Then I will! This man, my dear Mrs. Reynolds, is none other than your beloved husband, Captain Harry Reynolds!

MARGARET
It isn't true!
(*She takes a step backwards, falters, and is supported by Dale.*)

CHIEF
(*to Dexter*)
You no say right! No one know for sure identity of criminal!

DEXTER
What do you mean? You told me yourself that he was Reynolds' height and build, and that he was wearing a Mountie uniform.

CHIEF
But me no say this man Captain Reynolds, because me no see face. No one see face. Man always wear mask. (*He bows to Margaret.*) Me beg humble pardon, white lady, for this intrusion. Me come to Cariboo only to see justice done. Me no accuse your husband, or any other man.

MARGARET
Thank you. You are very kind. Well gentlemen, is this your reason for coming and scaring an innocent woman in the middle of the night?

DALE

I'm afraid that in spite of what the Chief says, Margaret, the police are certain that Harry did commit the crimes. Cariboo is the only Mountie station for miles, and we have received no reports of missing men. Our description of the desperado tallies perfectly with Harry's description. Why, one of the Indians even reported that the man carried a handkerchief with Harry's initials on it.

MARGARET

And I suppose Harry is the only person in Canada with those initials. What kind of proof is that?

DALE

Proof enough to arrest him, I'm afraid.

MARGARET

And you call yourself a friend!

DALE

You know if there's one person in the world I don't want to hurt it's you.

MARGARET

You've chosen a strange way of showing it.

DALE

Listen to me, Margaret! In spite of the fondness I have for you, you know I've always been Harry's friend too! Harry and I grew up together... went to school together... We used to go fishing and hunting together. Why, he's almost as dear to me as you are. You can be sure that if there's any way of saving him, I'll do my darnedest to prove his innocence. Meanwhile, it's my duty to arrest him and see that he comes back here to Cariboo to stand trial.

MARGARET
(*fixing him with a look*)
In view of the circumstances, *Lieutenant* Dale, I have nothing further to say to you.

DALE

But, Meg! I—

MARGARET

I said, that will do!

DALE
(*stiffening*)
Very well, ma'am. (*to the Chief*) Chief, I understand you are starting the journey back to Reindeer settlement tonight. Is that correct?

CHIEF

Ugh.

DALE

Then would you mind stopping at my office on your way out of town? There are a few minor details of the man's appearance I would like to go over with you.

CHIEF
(*bowing*)

Ugh.

DALE

Thanks for your cooperation. (*to everyone except Margaret*) Good night. (*He goes out.*)

DEXTER
(*to Margaret*)
So you still refuse to listen to reason, eh?

MARGARET

Mr. Dexter, you've been very kind to us since Harry left. I would hate to order you out of here the way I just did Lieutenant Dale.

DEXTER

I told you a long time ago your husband was no good.

MARGARET

Please!

DEXTER

Well, O.K., if you want to be stubborn. But just remember, you've always got a friend in Sam Dexter.

MARGARET

That's nice of you, but—

DEXTER

I heard what he was saying, just now, about being a friend of you and your husband. I'll be blunt, ma'am. I never did much care for your husband. It's you I like.

MARGARET

Really . . .

DEXTER

I know, I shouldn't be talking like this to a married woman, especially with people around. I don't care, see? Sam Dexter can buy and sell this town and he don't give a damn what people think. At least . . . except for one.

MARGARET

But can't you understand that I—

DEXTER

Say, how about us getting hitched? You could easily get a divorce from Reynolds *in absentia* after what he's done. I ought to know—I'm the judge of this town.

MARGARET

And now I must ask you to leave, Mr. Dexter. As you point out, I am a married woman, and I do not listen to proposals from other men. And

THE COMPROMISE 41

no man who is my true friend would make such a proposal. Let me also remind you that my husband Harry is *innocent* of any crime. Right now he is doing his duty, looking for the man who murdered your partner, Mr. Stevenson.

DEXTER

You sure have got a lot of spunk. I like that in a gal. (*Margaret goes to the door, opens it, and points outside.*) Before I go ma'am, I'd like to have just one word with my man here, Lucky Seven.
(*He leads Lucky Seven to the front of the stage. Margaret closes the door and talks to the Chief. The Indians are examining the various furnishings of the house. Dexter talks to Lucky Seven in an undertone.*)
You bonehead! You had to wear that mask when you were robbing the Indians, didn't you!

LUCKY SEVEN

Ugh, Mr. Dexter, Lucky Seven no look like Captain Reynolds in the face. Anyway, Tobi Indians know Lucky Seven—would report to Dale. Mister Dexter no want me go to jail, do him?

DEXTER

Jail's too good for you, you polecat. You'd sell your own grandmother for enough wampum, wouldn't you?

LUCKY SEVEN
(*joyfully*)

Ugh!

DEXTER

Well, you'll get enough if you do as I tell you. And no bungling this time! I thought the rumors about the dancing girl and the crimes you committed would be enough to make this shrinking violet forget about her husband, but it seems I'll have to resort to stronger measures. When I leave, I want you to go find that cross-eyed girl friend of yours, see?

LUCKY SEVEN
(*mournfully*)

Ugh!

DEXTER

Do you still have the handkerchief with the initials on it that you stole off her clothesline? (*Lucky Seven slily pulls the handkerchief part way out of his pocket.*) Good. When you see her, get her to brew you both some tea and then slip this pill (*handing him a pill*) into hers, get me? After you go I want you wait around outside until she starts snoring. Then you come back, plant the handkerchief somewhere in the room, and grab the kid.

LUCKY SEVEN
(*apprehensively*)

Me grab . . . kid?

DEXTER

You're catching on. Then get the hell out of Cariboo—my fastest dog team is waiting outside, in the woods just east of the house. Lay low for three weeks and then come back—say you've been visiting relatives up north. Oh—I almost forgot. Here's a little something for your traveling expenses. (*Lucky Seven looks into the bag Dexter hands him, rolls his eyes delightedly, and again looks apprehensive.*) And remember—you get three times that when you return to Cariboo.

LUCKY SEVEN

But what about . . . kid?

DEXTER

Knowing what sensitive feelings you have, I don't insist that you kill him. Fix him a nice soft bed in the wilderness—maybe the good fairies will take care of him. (*He continues half to himself.*) She'll think her husband has taken the kid to raise him up to be a crook like his dad—I hope! If this doesn't make her think he's no good, I give up. But what am I

THE COMPROMISE

saying? As if Sam Dexter could ever give up! (*sarcastically, turning to the others*) Excuse me, ladies and gentlemen! Sorry I can't remain longer in such charming company. Say, watch out for her, Chief—she's got a wicked tongue. Yes sir, a lot of spunk!
(*He goes out, laughing.*)

CHIEF
If Mrs. Reynolds pardon Chief speak, him think some of her neighbors in Cariboo not so nice.

MARGARET
Oh, he's a good man at heart, I guess. It's just that his manner is a little uncouth.

CHIEF
Indians have a saying—"Can tell color of panther's heart by color of his hide."

MARGARET
I'm so friendless and alone since Harry left. And Dexter has been kind . . . in his way. He's never asked for anything in return—until tonight.

LUCKY SEVEN
Excuse me, missus, am Mooka here?

MARGARET
Yes, you'll find her in the kitchen. (*He goes out.*) Will it always be thus?

CHIEF
Surely pain is long . . . almost as long as time.

MARGARET
Then there is more in store for me?

CHIEF
Every man has his full share of pain—and then some.

MARGARET

But I have lived through enough!

INDIANS

You have indeed deserved better than you have gotten.

MARGARET

And can you see no brightness ahead?

CHIEF

As we left camp the fortune-teller was casting his lots. He said a great day is coming—a day whose radiance will be to the present as day is to night.

MARGARET

And I—perhaps I may share in that day?

INDIANS

We hope so, lady.

MARGARET

Perhaps the lovely springtime will come for me too. Spring can be lovely in the wilderness. It was April, I remember, when Harry and I were wed. We rode on horseback through the woods. There were beautiful flowers growing all around—little flowers that bloom and fade away in less than a day. And I thought our love would last a lifetime, in spite of its sweetness. How wrong I was!

INDIANS

Do not torture yourself, lady. Our lot, too, is hard. Yet we bear it in silence.

MARGARET

I won't be silent! Nobody knows how I've suffered all these months! Spring passed, and summer, and autumn with red leaves. And now winter sits on my heart, as it did the day he went away. Oh frozen

THE COMPROMISE 45

mountain streams! barren crags! wolves of the wild timber! None of you is so cold, so cynical as my husband's heart.

CHIEF

Surely, in all these months, your heart has known some lightness?

MARGARET

None.

CHIEF

He left you without one consolation?

MARGARET

No . . . not one.

CHIEF

Then whose is that baby I see in the cradle over there?

MARGARET

Oh . . . my son! (*She gets him from the cradle.*) The sole warmth of his mothers' heart—her only joy! It's bad luck to have forgotten him at such a time! What if I were to lose him?

CHIEF

Rest assured, no harm will ever befall your son. I noticed him when I first came in—such brightness seemed to shine around him that I thought him the tomorrow of which our fortune-teller spoke.

MARGARET

Look—a tear on his little cheek. Perhaps he too misses his father.

CHIEF

Perhaps so. And now it is getting late, and we must go. But first, let me grant my blessing to this child, and to you too for having spoken kindly to us. (*Margaret kneels before him with her son.*) May the great raven who lives in the sunset look kindly on this baby and bring him up to be as great-hearted as he is. Let him always look after the rights of others, and live so as to be a joy to his mother, in the manner of men—for, living so, no evil can ever touch him. And may the raven look kindly also on this mother, and bring her happiness at last.

INDIANS

And may he look kindly also on her husband, and bring him back safely from wherever duty has taken him. For it is a sad thing for a woman to live without her husband.

MARGARET
(*rising*)

Thank you—you have been very good to us.

CHIEF

Don't speak of it. We see your gratitude in your face.

MARGARET

Will you pass this way again?

CHIEF

We have no plans to, but many unforeseen things happen.

MARGARET

Yes—perhaps we will meet again some day. I hope so.

CHIEF

So do we. Goodbye.
(*They all bow to Margaret and the Chief kisses her hand.*)

MARGARET

Goodbye.
(*The Chief and the Indians go out. Margaret puts the baby in his cradle, takes a lamp from the table and goes toward a door at the back, turning to look at the cradle.*)
"And no harm will ever befall him." Pleasant dreams, my dearest!
(*Mooka opens the kitchen door.*)

THE COMPROMISE

MOOKA

Will Missus wantum anything else?

MARGARET

No thank you, Mooka. I'm going to bed.
(*She goes off. Mooka signals to Lucky Seven.*)

MOOKA

Her go to bed. Come on—we sittum in living room like white missus and master.

LUCKY SEVEN
(*entering*)

O.K. First me sittum one side of fireplace and you serve me cup of tea.

MOOKA

Like this?

LUCKY SEVEN

Ugh. Now you sittum other side and drinkum tea.

MOOKA

No—first you gotta give me kiss.

LUCKY SEVEN

No—you drinkum tea, then me give kiss.

MOOKA
(*picks up a stick of wood and brandishes it*)

You givum me kiss now—O.K.?

LUCKY SEVEN

Well—O.K.
(*Mooka flops down on his lap and bends over backwards for the kiss. Lucky Seven drops the pill in her teacup and kisses her.*)

MOOKA

Now we sittum and talkum like white man and missus.

LUCKY SEVEN

What we talk about?

MOOKA

Let's talk about—getting married!

LUCKY SEVEN

What make you think we getting married?

MOOKA

But—you say we engaged!

LUCKY SEVEN

Exactly—so how we get married unless we breakum off engagement?

MOOKA

But how we get married if we not engaged?

LUCKY SEVEN

We don't! (*Mooka starts to cry.*) Don't cry, little papoose, maybe we do get married soon.

MOOKA

That better! When?

LUCKY SEVEN

Maybe when Lucky Seven get back from trip up north.

MOOKA

You takum trip? But you promised to takum me to big Indian dance next Saturday night!

LUCKY SEVEN

Lucky Seven just learn tonight his rich uncle in north sick, asking to see Lucky Seven. Maybe him die, leave Lucky Seven fortune so Lucky Seven marry Mooka.

MOOKA

You think so?

LUCKY SEVEN

It possible—Uncle rich man—Got plenty wampum.

MOOKA

Oh boy! Mooka no longer have to work! Her become nice lady like white missus.

LUCKY SEVEN

And Lucky Seven bring back present from north—maybe nice bearskin jacket.

MOOKA
(tenderly)

Ugh. Mooka like Lucky Seven.

LUCKY SEVEN

Me gotta go. Gotta gettum early start. First me drinkum up tea, then go. (*He drinks his.*) How come you no drink?

MOOKA

You give me goodnight kiss first, then me drink.

LUCKY SEVEN

No. You drinkum first, or no kiss. And no present from the north.

MOOKA

Aw . . . All right, but you old sourpuss just the same.
(*She drinks the tea, then bends over backwards as before. Lucky Seven holds her for a moment, then lets her fall to the floor.*)

LUCKY SEVEN

Twenty-three skiddoo! Ha ha ha!
(*He runs out. Mooka starts to chase him with a stick of wood, then returns to her chair by the fire.*)

MOOKA

Why Mooka ever trust him? Him bad Indian, that's what. Mooka no marry him now even if he ask her. Why him decide to go away so

suddenly? Funny him never mention rich uncle before. Ho hum. Mooka so sleepy, take little nap by fire before go-um to bed. Lucky Seven him act strangely lately. Zzzzz. Him seem to know lot about Captain Harry. Who tell him? Zzzzz. Maybe him know something about murder of Mr. Stevenson, too. Me remember to ask him. Zzzz. Oh, Mooka so sleepy, so very sleepy.
(*She falls asleep. In a moment, Lucky Seven, who has been watching through the window, steals in noiselessly, lifts the baby out of the cradle, drops the handkerchief next to it, and hurries out. The baby starts to cry just as they go out.*)
Zzzzz. No cry no more, Lucky Seven. Mooka be nice to you—maybe she even let you give her kiss. (*She wakes up with a start.*) Ugh, that no Indian man, it little Jim. (*She goes over to the cradle.*) Whattum matter, baby? Did him wettum cradle . . . ? Him gone! Jim! Jim! Him gone. (*She rushes to the outside door, calls out, and runs back to the center of the stage.*) Oh missus! Police! Help! Little Jim gone! Help! The baby gone! Help! Police!
(*Dexter enters.*)

DEXTER

What is it? I was just passing by the house on my way home from the store and I heard you making all this noise.

MOOKA

Him gone! Baby Jim! And him in his cradle only a minute ago! Help! Police!

DEXTER

Are you sure he isn't around the house someplace?

MARGARET
(*entering in a kimono*)
What is it, Mooka? Why are you yelling?

MOOKA

Oh Missus! Baby Jim! I see him in cradle only a minute ago!

MARGARET

What's happened to my baby?

MOOKA

Him gone!

MARGARET

Good heavens! Where? (*She sees Dexter.*) What are you doing here?

DEXTER

I heard all the noise and came to see if I could be of any help.

MARGARET

Well, why are you waiting? Go and find Lieutenant Dale! And hurry!

DEXTER

Just a minute, ma'am! Aren't you forgetting that you gave the Lieutenant his walking papers a short while ago, and in no uncertain terms?

MARGARET

What difference does that make? He's a police officer, isn't he? I'll go myself.

DEXTER

My dear! I'm as upset as you are, but you don't see me losing my head. I'm trying to decide on the best possible course of action.

MARGARET

Are you crazy? Go after the kidnapper!
(*Lieutenant Dale enters, with the Chief and the Indians.*)

DALE

What is it? What is the meaning of these screams?

MARGARET

Oh Lieutenant! I'm so glad to see you.

DALE

Indeed?

MARGARET

Please forgive me for my rudeness just now. But I know you will when you hear the terrible news. My baby has been kidnapped!

DALE

Kidnapped! But are you sure?

MARGARET

There's his empty cradle. What more proof do you want?

DALE

I see the cradle. Tell me, have you searched the house thoroughly?

MARGARET

Don't be ridiculous. Where could he go? I tell you, the child has been kidnapped!

MOOKA

He right, Lieutenant. Mooka say goodnight to her boy friend, Lucky Seven, then sit by fire and fall asleep. When her wake up, Jim gone!

DALE

But there are no strangers in town, and who among us would want to kidnap little Jim?

MARGARET

Whoever it was can't have gotten very far. Oh, won't somebody go after him? *(to the Indians)* What about some of you? Can't you go? *(to the Chief)* And you—what kind of a blessing was that you put on my child?

CHIEF
(bowing)

Indians try to do everything in their power to help white lady.

DALE

Before doing anything we must search the house for clues. It would be useless to set off into the woods at night without some idea of where to look.

THE COMPROMISE

MARGARET

While you waste time my baby is probably freezing to death.

DALE

No—see, the kidnapper seems to have taken all the blankets from the cradle. That's certainly a good sign.

AN INDIAN
(*bending over to pick up the handkerchief*)

Lookum, Lieutenant. Me find this on floor beside cradle.

DALE

A handkerchief—left behind by the kidnapper—and bearing the initials "H.R."

ANOTHER INDIAN

It just like one of masked man who attack our village.

MARGARET

That's Harry's handkerchief! I'd know it anywhere—I embroidered those initials myself.

DALE

I'm afraid this looks bad for Harry, Margaret.

MARGARET

Merciful heaven! But . . . you don't think he would kidnap his own son?

DALE

It certainly looks that way.

MARGARET

But why would he want to do such a thing?

DEXTER

Perhaps he wants to bring him up in his own way . . . to be a crook.

MARGARET

Bring up a baby? Alone and in the wilderness?

DEXTER

Perhaps . . . he's not alone.

DALE

Our reports say that Harry has gotten mixed up with a woman, Margaret. It's one aspect of the case I'd hoped to keep from you.

MARGARET

Then all those rumors I've heard are true! The pieces are falling into place at last. Harry's found a new love—a dancer, with expensive tastes, who makes him steal to support her. They've gone off together to live in the wilderness, and now that Harry's settled down he wants little Jim.

DALE

Easy, Margaret. Don't cry.

MARGARET

I can't help it! What kind of a mother will she make? What kind of a father will he be, for that matter? Raising our son to be a criminal!

It's all so clever, so very clever! When Jim's a little older he'll be able to go along with Harry on his burglaries, he'll climb in buildings and things like that. And no one will ever suspect Harry because he'll have a little boy with him. And then they'll go home to wherever they're hiding out from the law, and that woman will beat Jim and send him to bed without any supper, and then she'll put her arms around Harry and love him. And where will I be while all this is going on? I'll be all alone, growing older in this miserable little town, and no one will ever love me again. It's too terrible to think about!

DALE

I don't agree with the part of your speech about no one ever loving you again. It will be easy for you to divorce Harry *in absentia* and marry

... the man of your choice. You know there are plenty of men in this town, Meg, who'd give their right arm just to sit next to you on a sleighride!

DEXTER

There certainly are! Say, Lieutenant, aren't you neglecting your duty? While you're talking to Mrs. Reynolds the criminal is escaping.

DALE

Er ... of course. Well, bye bye, Margaret, and don't take on so.

MARGARET

Goodbye, Allan.
(*He leaves.*)

DEXTER

Well, I don't mean to rub it in but perhaps now you'll listen to me when I tell you a person's no good.

MARGARET

Don't, Mr. Dexter. Haven't I borne enough for one evening?

DEXTER

You wouldn't have had to if you'd taken my advice. Oh, Margaret, won't you divorce him and marry me?

MARGARET

Let's not talk about it tonight. I'm confused. I can't think straight.

DEXTER

You mean you'd stay married to that sneak after what he's done to you?

MARGARET

Harry's not a bad man, at heart. Whatever he's done, you can bet it's because that woman made him do it.

DEXTER

But you will divorce him?

MARGARET

Of course. How could I go on being married to him now?

DEXTER

And marry me?

MARGARET

I don't know. I can't think that far ahead.

DEXTER

No one could ever love you as I do, Margaret. If you marry me I'll build you the most beautiful home for miles around, with all the latest conveniences and a maid to wait on you hand and foot. Your name will be a legend all over northern Canada. You'll be called the Queen of Cariboo.

MARGARET

As far as a maid goes, Mooka here will, I hope, always be my loving and devoted servant. As for the other things, you can forget them. All I want is the love of a good and honest man.

DEXTER

You'll have all that and more. Then you do say yes?

MARGARET

I don't know, perhaps so . . . I'll think about it. Just now I feel a little faint.

DEXTER

(to Mooka)

Bring her some water. *(Mooka fetches a glass of water and gives it to Margaret, who drinks it.)* I can start the divorce proceedings tomorrow and you can be picking out your trousseau from the catalogue. We can be married within the month. What do you say?

MARGARET

Oh, what can I say? You've been so kind. Very well, Mr. Dexter, I will marry you.

THE COMPROMISE

DEXTER

You've made me the happiest man in the world!

CHIEF

Congratulations, Mr. Dexter. You gettum good wife.

DEXTER

A good wife? I'll say so! Oh boy! (*aside*) If only that meathead husband of hers doesn't come back and queer things before the wedding. After that, I don't care what happens. There'll be no getting rid of me then! (*aloud*) I'll give a big wedding reception, Chief, and invite you and your whole tribe.

CHIEF

Ugh. Me thank you, but afraid us cannot come. Reindeer settlement many miles away.

DEXTER

Well, just as you say.

CHIEF

But Mrs. Reynolds will be always in our thoughts. On wedding day we think of her and you, and drink special toast.

DEXTER

That's real nice of you.

CHIEF

And we pray always to raven god, that he watch over and protect her little son Jim.

MARGARET

Thank you! I'm sorry I spoke angrily to you a few moments ago.

CHIEF

You are forgiven. Life is so full of bitterness that we must speak out in anguished protest now and then.

MARGARET

And my life especially. Well, perhaps my forthcoming marriage will be a happy one.

INDIANS

I asked the snow, that falls continually on our frozen northern wastes, whether he had ever seen any of this happiness of which you speak. And the snow replied, truly, if there is any happiness in the world, only the dead know it. Still, we continue to hope that you will be happy.

DEXTER

It is a strange thing—we spend all our lives looking for it, yet deep down we know we will never find it. Even I, ever ruthless in my pursuit of power and money, know secretly that the quest is hopeless.

CHIEF

Then you are a wiser man than I took you for. Indeed, to realize that the quest is hopeless is the first step toward happiness.

DEXTER

How is that so? You speak in riddles.

CHIEF

True happiness comes only when we forget our own selfish desires and try to make others happy. That is the meaning of the word "happiness."

DEXTER

I know it, yet can't forget my ambitions, even for a minute.

MARGARET

Nor can I! Just now I was thinking of my own fate when my baby, my dear child, was stolen. Supposing it wasn't his father, but somebody even worse, who took him?

INDIANS

Have no fear, lady. The raven god is a good god, though his ways often seem inscrutable. He will watch over your son.

MARGARET

I hope so. Listening to your voices I can almost believe in your strange god.

INDIANS

Great is the power of the raven who dwells in the sunset. Fierce is he in battle, but gentle and meek as a lamb toward those he loves. Strange are his ways—often he seems to forget, yet he remembers. Always he watches over and protects those who believe in him.

MARGARET

Oh mighty god of the Indians! I too will believe in you if you will save my baby from harm!

CHIEF

The raven sees. He hears. He will watch over your son and smile on your marriage.

MARGARET

And I will never forget him in my happiness.

CHIEF

And now we must take leave of you for the second time tonight. For our way lies westward, through moonlit pine forests and trackless, snow-covered wastes.

DEXTER

I'm going too, Chief. I'll show you and your Indians the way to the edge of town.

INDIANS

We leave our hearts behind in this cabin, glad that some happiness has come to you, hoping that more will—and that sorrow will go away entirely. And so, good night.

CHIEF AND DEXTER

Good night!

MARGARET

Good night—and thanks!
(*Margaret and Mooka wave to Dexter, the Chief, and the Indians as they file slowly out into the snow.*)

CURTAIN

ACT II

Inside the Chief's tent at Reindeer settlement. At the back, a flap of the tent is open, revealing a sentry standing guard, white snow, and blue sky. At the right of the opening is an upright piano and, next to it, a glowing brazier. At the right of the stage is a curtained entrance to another room. The time is late afternoon. Harry Reynolds is talking with the Chief's two sons, Running Deer and Mountain Lion.

HARRY

And you say this man who has been robbing the settlement is about my height and build?

RUNNING DEER

Ugh, he your height and build, Captain Harry, but he no have same color hair. You have dark brown hair—him hair black and greasy, like Indian.

MOUNTAIN LION

Ugh—and him coloring different, too. Me see back of his neck and hands—and them dark, like skin of Indian.

RUNNING DEER

Also, him try to disguise voice. But me thinkum him have Indian accent.

HARRY

Do you think it could have been anyone in your father, the Chief's, tribe?

THE COMPROMISE

RUNNING DEER

No, we checkum on all braves at time of his visits—they all have alibis. Besides, no Tobi brave would ever act in this way.

HARRY

Do you have any ideas about who it might be?

RUNNING DEER

From color of hair, skin, and accent, me thinkum him Oomi Indian, from tribe north of Cariboo.

MOUNTAIN LION

Me too!

HARRY

That's where I come from. I know almost all the Indians in that neighborhood and not one of them has ever been arrested on any charge. They're peaceable and home-loving. Maybe there are one or two who occasionally take a little too much firewater ... But that wouldn't explain the presence of an Oomi in these parts, or the stolen Mountie uniform. No, there is some deeper motive for all this.

MOUNTAIN LION

That what Chief, my father, him say! Him think criminal only want to make it look like robbery since he take nothing of any value. Chief say he think man commit crimes to get other man in trouble.

HARRY

Your father is a smart man, Mountain Lion.

MOUNTAIN LION

Thank you, Captain Harry. By the way, Captain, who is that beautiful blonde who came here with you but who not get out of sled?

HARRY

You Indian braves have keen eyesight. That "beautiful blonde" as you call her is Miss Daisy Farrell, of Elk City, *chanteuse* and devotee of the terpsichorean art.

RUNNING DEER

Me no understand last part of sentence.

HARRY

Neither do I, Running Deer! That's the way she describes herself. Actually she's an entertainer at the Glass Slipper Saloon in Elk City.

MOUNTAIN LION

Me understand! She do bump—like this!
(*He imitates a belly dancer.*)

HARRY
(*laughing*)

Well, that's not quite it, but you're close.

RUNNING DEER

How come she travel with you, Captain? You needum extra warmth for these chilly nights?

HARRY

No, it's not that. I'm married, and appearances are deceiving in Daisy's case. Her hair may be bleached, but her heart is pure gold and it's in the right place. She's a good girl, and what's more she's got brains enough to stay that way.

She's here strictly on business—my business, that is. I've been on the trail of a killer for the last year. I traveled here not only to investigate the robberies, but also to see if there might not be a clue to connect the two criminals—the man who robbed your settlement, and the murderer of old Walter Stevenson.

THE COMPROMISE 63

RUNNING DEER

Me hear about murder. Him partner of Mr. Dexter of Cariboo, isn't that true?

HARRY

That's right. They ran an extremely profitable fur business—at least it *was* profitable until the furs started disappearing.

MOUNTAIN LION

Disappearing?

HARRY

Yes—three times in one winter a driver set out for Elk City with the furs—and three times the driver, the sled, and the furs vanished into thin air.

RUNNING DEER

And then—didn't Old Man Stevenson set out with the furs himself?

HARRY

He did, Running Deer. He wanted to find out who was stealing the furs, and he met . . . death.

MOUNTAIN LION

And Miss Farrell—she have clue to murder?

HARRY

We hope so. She was a friend of the Stevenson family, and went to the same school in the east as Mr. Stevenson's daughter. She knows about some personal disputes in the family, and has given me a pretty good idea of who the killer is, though of course I'm not at liberty to reveal it.

RUNNING DEER

Mountain Lion and me, we hope you findum, and we know our father the Chief, him hope so too. Him away in Cariboo right now, to tell Lieutenant Dale about the robberies. When him come back, him maybe give you some new clues.

HARRY

Thanks, Running Deer. We need all the help we can get.

MOUNTAIN LION

Captain Harry, how come you no ask Miss Daisy to come into wigwam with you?

HARRY

Well, I asked her to, but she's a little shy before strange men.

MOUNTAIN LION and RUNNING DEER

Ho! Ho! Ho!

HARRY

What are you laughing at?

MOUNTAIN LION and RUNNING DEER

You say her shy with strange men—but we only two Indian braves—and she sing and dance every night before big male audience at Glass Slipper.

HARRY

But that's different—when you're an entertainer on stage, you feel everyone in the audience is your friend.

MOUNTAIN LION

Then why not have her pretend Running Deer and me her audience? She sing for us, and she think us her friends. But first we all smokum peace pipe and then we make her honorary member of tribe, so she *know* we her friends.

HARRY

Why, that sounds like a wonderful idea. I know she'd be delighted to. (*He goes to the outside opening of the tent and calls.*) Oh Daisy! Daisy! My friends want to meet you!
(*Daisy enters. She is an attractive, husky-voiced blonde and wears a parka.*)

THE COMPROMISE

RUNNING DEER

Welcome to our humble tent, Miss Farrell.

MOUNTAIN LION

We very honored that you visit us.

DAISY

Hiya, boys. Pleased to meet you, I'm sure. What did you say your names were?

RUNNING DEER

Me Running Deer.

DAISY

Running Deer. I had a boy friend once that should have been named that.

MOUNTAIN LION

And me Mountain Lion.

DAISY

That's a pretty name too. Tell me, are you that fierce? (*Mountain Lion roars.*) O.K., O.K., I believe you. (*looking around*) This is quite a place you have here. A fur rug, a piano, central heating, even a doorman—and no windows to wash. Say, do you have special weekly rates?

MOUNTAIN LION

For you, we charge . . . nothing!

RUNNING DEER

You can stay as long as you like . . . free!

DAISY

Now, wait a minute. Let's not rush things.

HARRY

No, they're serious, Daisy. They want to make you an honorary member of their tribe.

DAISY

Me . . . a squaw? But then I'd have to carry you around on my back. On second thought, maybe I should accept. I was once told I have a face like a tomahawk. Seriously, boys, I'm very touched and I'd love to join your tribe.

RUNNING DEER and MOUNTAIN LION

Ugh!

DAISY

Oh, well, if you're going to get cold feet about it.

RUNNING DEER

First we present you with ceremonial headdress and wampum necklace. Then we all smokum peace pipe together.

MOUNTAIN LION

Here necklace.

DAISY

Ugh—I mean, thank you. This goes around my neck, you say? (*She puts it on and examines a tag attached to it.*) "Made in Brooklyn!" Are you sure this isn't one of those "Add-a-Wampum" necklaces?

RUNNING DEER

And here headdress.

DAISY
(*trying it on*)

Well, this is more like it. Gosh, I haven't felt this way since I toured Manitoba in the Follies.

HARRY

You really do look stunning, Daisy.

DAISY

I'll bet you tell that to all the squaws!

RUNNING DEER

And now we all smokum peace pipe. (*He hands the pipe to Daisy.*) Here, puff!

DAISY

(*She takes a puff and coughs violently.*)

Do you have one with a filter tip?
(*She hands it to Harry who smokes and coughs.*)

HARRY
(*coughing*)

It's delicious.

DAISY

Peace pipe! Remind me not to ask you to show me any of your war dances.
(*The two Indians have been laughing uproariously at the coughing. Now Mountain Lion starts to smoke and cough, and hands the pipe to Running Deer, who also coughs. The sentry has come in to watch, and laughs. They hand him the pipe and soon everyone is coughing violently and the wigwam fills up with smoke.*)

RUNNING DEER

Me no understand! Prince Albert never taste like that before.

MOUNTAIN LION

Me have confession, Running Deer. Me buy big can of other tobacco from travelling salesman. He say it just as good, and only half the price.

SENTRY

It taste like sawdust to me.

RUNNING DEER

Well, let's gettum on with ceremony. Now that we all smokum pipe of peace, it gives great pleasure to me, Running Deer, son of the Chief of the Tobi Indians—

MOUNTAIN LION

And me, Mountain Lion, also his son—

BOTH

—to welcome you to the Tobi tribe as an honorary squaw, with all the rights and privileges thereof—including the right of marrying into the tribe and settling here, should you ever so desire.

MOUNTAIN LION

And we sure hope you *do* desire . . . some day!

DAISY

I'm all choked up. I never realized how nice it feels to be a squaw—at least, now that the initiation is over, it does.

RUNNING DEER

And now that you our friend, and are no longer shy with us, maybe you sing us one of your songs, huh?

MOUNTAIN LION

We love to hear you sing.

DAISY

I'm a little out of voice, but . . . since you boys have been so nice . . . sure, I'd be glad to coöperate. Could I have a chord?
(*The sentry sits at the piano and accompanies. Daisy sings:*)

> From the Yukon to the Arctic Circle
> Everybody's in a whirl.
> All through the North Woods everybody's talking
> About a single girl.
>
> Nobody knows where she came from
> And no one knows where she'll go,
> But they say she lights up those North Woods
> Like the moonlight on the snow.

She wasn't wearing a parka
When she came into town;
No, she wasn't wearing a fur coat,
But a beautiful white satin gown.

All of the Mounties know her—
She singles them out one by one.
And lonely trappers know her,
But she gives her heart to none.

Her heart is as cold as the icicles
That form in the winter nights;
And she'll never say "I do" to you, my boy,
For her name is Miss Northern Lights.

All through those cold old North Woods
Hearts are in a whirl;
No one can sleep in the North Woods,
Dreamin' 'bout a single girl.

(*Harry and the Indians applaud vigorously. During the latter part of the song the Chief and his Indians appeared and have been standing in the opening of the wigwam, watching.*

RUNNING DEER

What a beautiful song!

HARRY

It certainly was, Daisy.

MOUNTAIN LION

Me likum too!

CHIEF

And me—my heart was likewise moved. But it sound to me as if song about you.

DAISY

Gee whiz! Standing room! You must be the Big Chief, Running Deer's and Mountain Lion's father.

CHIEF

That me. But who are you?

DAISY

I'm a friend of Captain Reynolds. We came here to investigate the robberies and a murder. But . . . er, won't you come in and make yourselves at home?

CHIEF

(*bowing and smiling*)

Me thank pretty white lady for kind invitation. (*They enter the tent.*) And you, Captain Reynolds, me glad to see you but me sorry also.

HARRY

How is that?

CHIEF

Me bringum bad news from Cariboo, me afraid.

HARRY

Quick! Is it about Margaret?

CHIEF

About her, and about somebody else too.

HARRY

Little Jim? What has happened to them—you must tell me!

CHIEF

Me make long story short. First, your wife get lonesome waiting for you. Then, she hear you been seeing another woman.

HARRY

But that's a lie! Daisy and I are just friends—we've been working on the case together.

DAISY

You do believe us, don't you, Chief?

CHIEF

Yes, but afraid me powerless to help situation. Anyway, rumor circulate around Cariboo that you the one who rob our settlement.

HARRY

It's incredible!

CHIEF

But Mrs. Reynolds no believum. Then Baby Jim kidnapped out of cradle, and police find your initialled handkerchief nearby. Everybody think you kidnapper—including Mrs. Harry. Now she going to divorce you before you get back and marry Mr. Dexter, owner of trading post.

HARRY
(bowing his head)

I just can't believe it.

CHIEF

Listen. You must hurry back to Cariboo. Their wedding only two weeks away, and it two weeks' journey from here to there. But be careful—order out for your arrest.

HARRY

Go back there now? Never!

DAISY

Harry, you must! Listen to what the Chief says.

CHIEF

If you don't go back, you lose wife and everybody think you a criminal.

HARRY

If Margaret has so little faith in me, she deserves to marry Dexter. I'll bet she invented those stories herself.

CHIEF

No, she try hard not to believe, but those around her try to persuade her.

HARRY

A likely story! No one could force her to turn against me if she didn't want to. No, Chief, I know you have a big heart, and hate to see anyone experience pain. But if there's one lesson I've learned in life it's this—to forget about those who desert you.

CHIEF

That not a good lesson. Often they come back, if we show we have faith in them.

DAISY

That's true, Harry.

HARRY

What do I care for your preaching! From now on I'm on my own—no one will ever tell me what to do! But why am I wasting my time here? I've got work to do.

CHIEF

What kind of work?

HARRY

To find little Jim, of course!

CHIEF

But others already look for him—it useless for you to go. Me think you do best to return to Cariboo!

HARRY

I'm sorry, Chief, but I can't believe that anyone else will try as hard to find him as I intend to. And Margaret shall never be my wife again.

THE COMPROMISE 73

CHIEF

It often happens, when we find one thing, we find others as well. You already looking for Stevenson murderer—maybe you should stick to first quest, and other things happen by themselves.

HARRY

I don't understand you! And I'm losing precious time. Chief, be kind enough to lend me some clothes to disguise myself. I'll be arrested on sight in this uniform.

CHIEF

Very well, my son. Perhaps some day you see folly of your ways, and return to right path. Mountain Lion, supply Captain Harry with new wardrobe. (*Mountain Lion leads Harry off to the right.*) It sad sight to see man fallen so low.

DAISY

Yes—you were so right in all your pronouncements.

CHIEF

It out of question for him to return to Elk City now that him marked man. Maybe you stay with us for few days until we sendum sled down for supplies?

DAISY

Why, I'd love to! I'm crazy about this place—everyone is so friendly. I'll bet you didn't know I've been made an honorary squaw.

CHIEF

Me know what happen when me see you in necklace and headdress. Me suspect Running Deer and Mountain Lion behind it all. They likum pretty ladies.

DAISY

They're sweet boys—and so is their father.
(*Harry and Mountain Lion return. Harry is now wearing an Indian costume, with a fur-trimmed hood.*)

HARRY

Thank you for your kindnesses, Chief. I should be able to get by in this disguise. I'm sorry if I spoke roughly just now. You are a good man, but I must do my duty as I see it. All men must.

CHIEF

Yes—even when they wrong about "duty."

HARRY

Are you coming, Daisy?

DAISY

No, I'm staying. You can't return to Elk City, and the Chief has kindly allowed me to exercise my prerogatives as a squaw for a few days.

HARRY

Then goodbye, all of you. I hope we may meet again on some more fortunate occasion.

INDIANS

Goodbye.

DAISY

Goodbye, Harry. (*He goes out. Daisy starts to cry.*) He's such a brave man—but so proud.

CHIEF

Yes. But do not weep over him. He is a fine man—things may yet work out all right for him. And now, you must be tired. Perhaps you would like to rest up a bit before supper, which is at seven o'clock in the main tent.

DAISY

Yes, that might be nice.

CHIEF

Running Deer, perhaps you will show—but what is your name? Boys, what name did you give her?

RUNNING DEER

We didn't have time to give her one, Father.

CHIEF

Then I shall name her myself. Let's see, what would be a good name? I have it—Miss Northern Lights!

INDIANS

Hooray! Hooray for Miss Northern Lights!

DAISY

It's a pretty name, but a very flattering one.

CHIEF

No, it suits you perfectly. Now, Running Deer, show Miss Northern Lights where her tent is. And then hurry back here, because I want you to give me an account of what's taken place in the camp since I've been away.

RUNNING DEER

Yes, Father.

DAISY

Until later, then.
(*They go out.*)

CHIEF

I think I'll just take a little nap before they get back.

MOUNTAIN LION

Yes, Father, you look rather tired. (*The Chief yawns and stretches, and then goes off to the right.*) Well, brothers, what did you find on your voyage over the mountains?

INDIANS

Little but snow, and barren rocks, and human desolation more uncongenial than these.

MOUNTAIN LION

So I thought from your faces. And here things haven't gone too well, either.

INDIANS

Why, what do you mean?

MOUNTAIN LION

I mean that our tribe is impoverished, as you know. And even worse than that, our pride is gone, too.

INDIANS

What signs of this have you seen?

MOUNTAIN LION

All around me I see lying, avarice, and petty bickering. I have seen our braves fighting over the seat nearest to the fire, or the last piece of meat in the dish. And our squaws go cold and hungry. Their husbands no longer care for them; they sit all day long at the tent opening, staring blankly at the sunlit ground. Most of our braves are engaged in bootlegging, illegal fur trading, and other shady deals in order to make a little money. And who can blame them? Even Running Deer and myself, who have done our best to keep the others in order, are sorely tempted to go and take jobs in Elk City.

But worse than poverty and degradation is the decay of the tribal spirit. Each begins to go his own way, no one thinks of the group any more, no one worships the old familiar gods. What is happening to us?

INDIANS

Truly, inside and outside our settlement, pain, death, poverty, and auguries of future unhappiness are everywhere, like the spirit of the great raven himself.

MOUNTAIN LION

Hush, my friends! Do not even dream of uttering a blasphemy!

INDIANS

For a long time the fortune-teller has been saying that a white child, born to one of our women, would lead us back from the brink of destruction. Well, where is this child? It was to have been born this year, and the year is almost over and not one of our wives is pregnant. Like all prophecies, this one is as vain and foolish as the god that inspired it.

MOUNTAIN LION

Oh, my friends, not you too! I fear what this may mean to our community.

INDIANS

Hasn't enough happened already? Why postpone the bitter end?

MOUNTAIN LION

You don't know what you're saying! Oh, if only some vision would guide me out of this pit into which I feel my spirit is sinking!

INDIANS

All visions are empty, vain, and foolish as the gods who inspire them.

MOUNTAIN LION
(bowing his head)

Perhaps . . . perhaps it is so.
(Blue Feather rushes in.)

BLUE FEATHER

Quick! Where is the Chief? I must speak to him at once!

MOUNTAIN LION

What is it? What is the matter with you?

BLUE FEATHER

The Chief! I must see the Chief!

MOUNTAIN LION

Whatever you have to say to him, Blue Feather, you can say to me. I am his son.
(*Running Deer enters.*)

RUNNING DEER

What is he doing here? I saw him come running in as if he owned the place.

BLUE FEATHER

You idiots! I tell you only the Chief shall hear my news.

CHIEF
(*entering*)

Well, what is it, Blue Feather? You know I always rest before dinner. Is this your way of welcoming me back?

BLUE FEATHER

Yes, O mighty Chief! Yes, it is. I have a gift for you, a wonderful gift. One that will lead our tribe back to its former prosperity!

CHIEF

That is certainly good news, if true.

BLUE FEATHER

It is true, I tell you!

CHIEF

Well, where is this gift?

BLUE FEATHER

It will soon be here. Oh, this is the happiest day of my life! To think that it is I, I who am to be the salvation of the Tobi tribe.

INDIANS
(*to each other*)

What is it? . . . What is he talking about? . . . I don't trust him . . . Neither do I . . . He has never done anything before to enhance our reputation . . . No, far from it.

THE COMPROMISE 79

CHIEF

Watch what you are saying, Blue Feather. If you indeed hold the secret of our salvation, it will be a great thing for the tribe and you. If you are lying, it could mean your disgrace and even permanent exile from us.

BLUE FEATHER
(*aside*)

Some punishment! (*aloud*) In one moment you will cease to doubt me.

SENTRY
(*entering*)

Great Chief, there is a nurse out here who wants to see you.

CHIEF

Show her in!
(*The sentry leads in a squaw carrying a white baby.*)

BLUE FEATHER

Now maybe you'll believe me. This, Chief and braves, is my son—*my white son*—whom my wife gave birth to scarcely an hour ago.

CHIEF

Is this true? I didn't even know your wife was pregnant.

SQUAW

It true, all right. Me deliver baby, myself. His wife no let on her pregnant, because her want to surprise husband.

RUNNING DEER

Then the prophecy has been fulfilled.

MOUNTAIN LION

The one the fortune-teller told us about!

INDIANS

Hooray! Hooray for Blue Feather!

BLUE FEATHER
Thank you, my friends.
CHIEF
Do you mind if I hold the child?
BLUE FEATHER
No, no! He's yours, in a sense.
CHIEF
(*aside, while Blue Feather talks with the others*)

A white child! The salvation predicted for our tribe? Surely it cannot be true! But why should I doubt it? Can I doubt the authority of the gods? Oh great raven, forgive my skepticism! But wait—I have seen this little one before—this is no new-born baby! It was back in Cariboo that I saw it, in its little cradle, watched over by its mother! It is Jim, the kidnapped child!

What am I to do now? Of course I must notify the mother—it will prove Harry's innocence, and prevent their divorce. But . . . will it? Margaret has already renounced her husband—he may have been right in taking a drastic view of her actions. And the kidnapper has not been found—maybe it was the father, for all I know.

And then, look at these smiling faces of my tribesmen. It would be the final blow to them if I were to expose this fraud. Perhaps I will wait a little while, till we get back on our feet, before telling the truth. Meanwhile if any serious problem arises owing to the child's disappearance, I can always come forward with the true story.

I know these are just excuses, but still I have a funny hunch that I am doing the right thing. If I didn't, the fate of my whole tribe couldn't deter me from making the facts known.

Now my course must be to watch, and wait, and hold my tongue, and try to find out how the baby got here—for thereby, I suspect, hangs an interesting tale. (*returning the child to Blue Feather*) Thank you for letting me see him. He's as handsome as one would expect a child sent from heaven to be.

BLUE FEATHER

Thanks, O Chief.
(*Daisy enters wearing a squaw costume.*)

DAISY

What's happened? It seems like everybody in the camp is running toward this tent. I thought it was an Elks' Convention.

CHIEF

My dear, you come to us at a fortunate time. Blue Feather's wife has just had a white baby, thus fulfilling a prophecy and saving us all from ruin.

DAISY

Gosh, that's swell!

CHIEF

And I think it would be fitting, since you are of the same race as this child, and since he belongs to the whole tribe, in a manner of speaking, if you were to take care of him for as long as you choose to stay with us, which we hope will be long indeed. That is, if Blue Feather and his wife have no objections.

BLUE FEATHER

Sure—anything.

DAISY

And I'd love to. (*taking the child*) He's certainly a cute little dickens.

CHIEF

I will rear him as my own son, and see that he is given every advantage, as befits our new leader.

INDIANS

Hooray! Hooray! Hooray!

CHIEF

Oh great raven, we thank you for your kindness to us! Grant us the prosperity you promised, and grant that in the future we may be able to lead lives free from deceit.

INDIANS

Hooray! Hooray for the raven!

RUNNING DEER

Come on, everybody, let's run to the mess hall and tell the others!

INDIANS

O.K.! Let's! Come on, everybody! Whoopee!
(*They all go out except for the Chief, Daisy, and the Squaw.*)

DAISY
(*to the Squaw*)

You stay. We'll fix him a nice warm bed by the fire . . . What's the matter, Chief? You seem troubled.

CHIEF

Me? Oh, it's nothing. I just hope everything turns out all right. I hate to see my braves disappointed in anything.

DAISY

They certainly didn't look very disappointed just now.

CHIEF

No—but hopes are sometimes dashed.

DAISY

Aw, don't be a worry bird. I have a feeling wonderful days are ahead.

CHIEF

Do you? I guess maybe they are. I hope so.

DAISY

I sure hope I'll be around to share in them.

CHIEF

Why won't you be?

DAISY

There's my job in Elk City. They're not going to hold it for me forever. And then, I couldn't go on sponging on your hospitality.

CHIEF

How would you like to stay on as . . . my wife?

DAISY

(*enthusiastically*)

Gosh, Chief, I'd love to!

CHIEF

I realize I haven't much to offer in the way of youth or good looks—

DAISY

Aw, cut it out, Chief! I'm about ready for the glue factory, myself.

CHIEF

—or material advantages—

DAISY

I love roots and berries!

CHIEF

I'm old enough to be your father—

DAISY

What difference does that make when true love is at stake? You have plenty to offer in the way of wisdom and experience, and that counts for more than you think with us girls. And anyway, you *are* cute. So there.

CHIEF

Now I know you're lying—

DAISY

I thought so the first minute I laid eyes on you!

CHIEF

Prove it!

DAISY

O.K.—you asked for it!
(*She kisses him.*)

CHIEF
(*to the Squaw, who has started to run out*)
Hey, where are you going?

SQUAW

Me be right back! Me gotta tell girl friend something!
(*She runs out. Daisy and the Chief look at each other, smile, laugh happily, and embrace as the curtain descends.*)

CURTAIN

ACT III

Five years later. The scene is the interior of Dexter's house in Cariboo—a large, high-ceilinged room with a fireplace, above which hang an Indian blanket and a rifle. There is a door on the right, and the outside door is on the left. Through a window at the back one can see a snowy scene, dotted with cabins, with dawn breaking over the mountains. Margaret is seated at a table, her head pillowed in her arms. Mooka, in a maid's uniform, enters from the kitchen.

MOOKA

Her been sitting there all night, me bet! (*She goes over to her.*) Wake up, missus! What you want to sleep here all night for?

MARGARET

(*She raises her head and blows out a lamp on the table.*)
You're wrong, I haven't been asleep.

MOOKA

Oh, what you wantum do it for? You ruining your health.

MARGARET

You know the answer to that question as well as I do, Mooka.

MOOKA

You waitum for no-good ex-husband to return?

MARGARET

No, I never want to see him again. I wouldn't have divorced him five years ago and married Mr. Dexter if I did. It's Jim—Baby Jim—I'm waiting for. I know he'll come back some day. That's why I wait every night at this window. I want him to be able to find his way to this house. (*Mooka stifles a sob.*) And I want you to promise me something. Mooka.

MOOKA
(*tearfully*)
You know Mooka do anything in her power for white missus.

MARGARET

If I should . . . go away, or something like that, I want you to promise that you'll always keep this lamp burning every night. Then I can be easy in my mind.

MOOKA

You no go away!

MARGARET

Yes, I'm afraid I am going away—to a convent.

MOOKA

A convent! No! White missus like life—gaiety—friends. She not find happiness in convent.

MARGARET

It's true I used to love life—in the glad days of my first marriage. But those times are gone forever. Now I have nothing to look forward to, except to pass the rest of my life in solitude, and to go to meet my Maker as soon as possible.

MOOKA

(*sinking to her knees before Margaret*)

No! Mooka never let you go!

MARGARET

I must.
(*Dexter enters.*)

DEXTER

Well, you're up nice and early. Is breakfast ready, Mooka?

MOOKA

It almost ready—me bring!
(*She goes out.*)

DEXTER

I hope you haven't been sitting up all night again, waiting for that brat of yours to return.

MARGARET

And if I have?

DEXTER

It won't do you any good, because even if he did come back I wouldn't let him in. Harry Reynolds' son will never enter this house.

MARGARET

Then I don't intend to stay in it either. As a matter of fact, I've made arrangements to enter the convent in Moose Junction. My things are packed—I'm leaving today. Lucky Seven has promised to drive me there.

DEXTER

Lucky Seven—ha! ha!—has promised—ha! ha! ha!

MARGARET

What's so funny?

DEXTER

Funny? Oh, nothing. (*He laughs some more.*) Well, have a nice trip. (*He starts to leave the room, still laughing.*)

MARGARET

(*She walks after him and seizes him by the arm.*)
Wait a minute! What are you laughing at?

DEXTER

(*grabbing her viciously*)

Now look here, my beloved wife! You're going nowhere, do you hear? Nowhere! You think Lucky Seven doesn't tell me everything you tell him, and a lot more? Then you're not as smart as I gave you credit for being.

MARGARET

It doesn't matter. If Lucky Seven won't drive me there, I'll find someone else who will.

DEXTER

You ain't findin' nobody! You're my wife and you're staying right here.

MARGARET

Your wife—as if you wanted a wife. You only married me because I wouldn't accept you at first—and it hurt your pride.

DEXTER

Maybe so, but that doesn't mean I'm lettin' you go. No sir, nobody walks out on Sam Dexter.

MARGARET

You can't keep me here.

DEXTER

I have ways of making you stay, and if you try to disobey me you'll find out what they are.

MARGARET

You're heartless!

DEXTER

And I'm also your legal husband—remember that the next time you think of leaving my bed and board.

MOOKA

(*entering with a tray*)

You want breakfast in here?

DEXTER

No, bring it in my den. I don't want to disturb Mother Superior at her devotions.

(*They go off at the right. Margaret sinks down at the table, her head pillowed on her arms, and weeps noiselessly. Mooka returns in a moment with a coffee pot.*)

MOOKA

Now, you drinkum coffee and not look so sad.

MARGARET

No thank you, I don't want anything.

THE COMPROMISE 89

MOOKA

No, you take—feel better. (*Margaret drinks.*) What him say to make missus sad this way?

MARGARET

He told me he won't let me go, Mooka. He's going to keep me here as a prisoner. He said Lucky Seven told him my plans.

MOOKA

No—Lucky Seven not do thing like that!

MARGARET

He said Lucky Seven tells him everything.

MOOKA

Lucky Seven not the best—but him good Indian! Him no stool pigeon. (*Margaret rests her forehead in her hands.*) Listen, Mooka talk to him, her get him to drive you to convent, if you want to go. Her twistum Lucky Seven around little finger—you gettum wish!

MARGARET

Thank you, Mooka. You always do look after me, don't you? I'll go now and finish packing my things. Try to speak to Lucky Seven as soon as possible—tell him I'll give him money—more than I'd promised—if he'll keep the secret.

MOOKA

He do it—and not for money, for Mooka!

MARGARET

I hope so!
(*She goes out. Mooka starts to hum and dust with a feather duster.*)

MOOKA

Lucky Seven probably not understand white missus wish to keep her plans from Mr. Dexter. Me remindum of duty to missus, and then he helpum. Him good Indian at heart. (*There is a knock at the door.*) Come in! (*Lucky Seven enters.*) My passion flower! Us was just talking about you.

LUCKY SEVEN

Hello, porcupine face.

MOOKA

Lucky Seven lovum joke! But why you tellum Dexter of white missus' plans?

LUCKY SEVEN

Because it my job, that why. But me no wanna listenum to you, Cross-eyes. Me gotta see Dexter.

MOOKA

Wait! Mooka promise you take missus to Moose Junction! You cannot lettum Mooka down!

LUCKY SEVEN

Me glad to takum her anywhere, if she can payum for ticket.

MOOKA

Ticket! How much?

LUCKY SEVEN

$10,000—in cash.

MOOKA

Ah! But missus no havum big money—even Dexter not got that much. You terrible Indian! Me tellum Lieutenant Dale you attempt extortion, and then see how far you gettum! Me go right now!

LUCKY SEVEN

You go nowhere, unless you want perforated hide.
(*He flashes a pistol.*)

MOOKA

A gun! And all the time me think you lovum Mooka! Me shoulda known!
(*She starts to cry.*)

LUCKY SEVEN
(*confused*)

Ugh, don't cry—me sorry. I mean—shut up or I'll shoot!
(*Dexter enters.*)

DEXTER

Oh, it's you. Put that pistol away. (*to Mooka*) You get into the kitchen and shut the door behind you. (*Mooka goes into the kitchen, but does not shut the door all the way and remains listening.*) I ought to brain you for flashing that illegal gat in here—you think I want every Mountie in these parts on my neck? What are you doing here, anyway? Did you bring me the payments for those furs?

LUCKY SEVEN

Me bringum bad news! Captain Reynolds on way back to Cariboo!

DEXTER

That's impossible—he wouldn't dare set foot in town. The Mounties have orders to shoot him on sight.

LUCKY SEVEN

Me glad you not scared.

DEXTER

Why should I be? There's nothing he can do to me—not even take his wife back, 'cause she's my wife now.

LUCKY SEVEN

Me almost forget—my Indian informant say Captain no longer care about wife—say you can have her.

DEXTER

That's sensible of him.

LUCKY SEVEN

Him come back to Cariboo only because him want to arrest you for murder of Mr. Stevenson and having me kidnap Baby Jim.

DEXTER

He's crazy! No one will believe I did it!

LUCKY SEVEN

But him always gettum man!

DEXTER

Shut up, you! (*He slaps him.*) That's just in case you ever think of squealing on me, which I know you wouldn't.

LUCKY SEVEN

Mr. Dexter! How can you thinkum such terrible thing about Lucky Seven?

DEXTER

Forgive me, my friend. I just wanted to remind you of your firm moral principles. Now, when is Reynolds due to arrive here?

LUCKY SEVEN

Me not know—maybe today, maybe tomorrow, maybe next week.

DEXTER

I want you to get your Indian pals to keep watch over all the approaches to town. The moment any stranger appears, have them report to me— understand?

LUCKY SEVEN

Ugh!

DEXTER

But first, go over to Mountie headquarters and tell that nice young Lieutenant Dale I'd like to say a few words to him in my private study concerning a certain notorious thief and kidnapper whose appearance in Cariboo is imminent.

LUCKY SEVEN

Me gottum!
(*He goes out.*)

DEXTER

I'll have Reynolds' hide yet! What a relief to be rid of that gum snowshoe after all these years! With him gone and that imbecile Dale head of the police force, I'll be ruler over the whole North Woods! If only Margaret doesn't get suspicious of me and tip Dale off.
(*He goes off at the right. Mooka enters.*)

MOOKA

So that what happen to old Mr. Stevenson! Him killed by Dexter! Lucky Seven kidnappum Baby Jim! Me thank stars me not consent when him wanta marry Mooka!

Me go tell Lieutenant Dale at once! Me not tell missus—if she find out she have hysterics and Dexter shoot her, maybe, when he see she know. Him dangerous criminal! Me go right now.
(*She starts for the door. Margaret enters.*)

MARGARET

Well, Mooka, have you spoken to Lucky Seven?

MOOKA

Uh—me not get chance to see him yet—me go right now and tell him.

MARGARET

You have talked to him, because I saw him coming up to the house from my bedroom window. What did he say? Never mind. I can read his answer in your face. He refused, didn't he?

MOOKA

Ugh—well . . .

MARGARET

He did, I can see. Well, I'll just have to think of some other way. If only Lieutenant Dale were still my friend. But he hasn't spoken to me since I married Mr. Dexter. Poor boy, how it must have hurt him!

MOOKA

Me go ask him now!

MARGARET

No, that wouldn't do. I've been cruel to him and I don't deserve his help. I must think of something else—of someone who would dare to defy Dexter and help me . . . (*She sighs.*) But there isn't anybody. Everybody else in this town is afraid of him, or they owe him too much money. (*Mooka is edging toward the door.*) Where are you going?

MOOKA

Me gottum go next door—borrow cup of sugar!

MARGARET

You can think of food at a time like this!

MOOKA

We gotta eat—keepum up strength.

MARGARET

Now, Mooka, you sit right down in that chair. There's no need for you to borrow a cup of sugar.

MOOKA

Oh—lettum me go! Please!

MARGARET

Not until you tell me what's on your mind—what's making you so jittery.

MOOKA

No, me can't tell. At least, not now!

MARGARET

I'm going to get to the bottom of this if we have to stay here all day! (*There is a knock at the door. Mooka starts to answer it.*) Never mind—I'll get it. You sit right where you are. (*The knock is repeated.*) On second thought, I think you'd better go into the kitchen and sit until you're ready to explain to me why you were so anxious to leave the house just now.

MOOKA

Me no wanna leave now! Me wanna stay here with you!

MARGARET

No, I want you to go into the kitchen as your punishment for being so secretive with me, your best friend. (*There is another knock. Mooka tries to go and answer it.*) Mooka!

MOOKA

But . . . Oh, all right!
(*She goes off.*)

MARGARET

Come in. (*Dale enters.*) Oh . . .
(*She turns her back on him, deeply moved.*)

DALE

I am here on your husband's orders.

MARGARET
(*not turning around*)

His room is . . . that way.
(*She points.*)

DALE

Thank you.
(*He starts toward the door at the right.*)

MARGARET

Are you . . .

DALE

Yes?

MARGARET

. . . sure you can find the way?

DALE

I think I can, thank you. (*He starts toward the door again and stops.*) Oh, Meg!

MARGARET
(*turning*)

Yes?

DALE

Why must we act this way, like total strangers?

MARGARET

I don't know! Life is so cruel!

DALE

Those words seem to have a special meaning for you.

MARGARET

Alas! It's true.

DALE

Then you haven't been happy all these years?

MARGARET

Happy? I don't even know the meaning of the word.

DALE

You don't know how happy it makes me to hear you say that.

MARGARET

Ever since my baby was stolen I haven't had a joyful moment.

DALE
(*stiffening*)

Oh . . . So that's the cause of your sorrow.

MARGARET

Oh, Allan, don't go on. Don't force me to say things about my marriage that I would regret later on.

DALE

Regret? . . . Then your marriage hasn't been happy?

MARGARET

It has been hell! He hasn't addressed a kind word to me since the minister pronounced us man and wife. I can't see my old friends . . . I can't even think about my baby. But I do! Every night—at this window. I keep a lamp burning for him, hoping somehow he'll find his way home.

DALE

My poor dearest!

MARGARET

Only today I was forbidden to leave the house! Oh, if only you could help me, Allan, I'd be so grateful!

DALE

I'll do everything in my power! Just tell me what I can do.

MARGARET

I must get away from this place. Even the thought of my child returning no longer deters me, especially since Mooka has promised to look after him if he comes. I want to enter a convent—there's one in Moose Junction. There seems no other way open to a bereft mother married to a heartless tyrant.

DALE

You are wrong. There is another way!

MARGARET

And what might that be?

DALE

You know that I have always loved you.

MARGARET

No—I mustn't listen.

DALE

But you must: it's too late for you not to listen! Do not renounce for the third and perhaps the last time the feeling that I know surges within you as it does within me! Oh, Margaret, say that you love me too!

MARGARET

It is true—I do love you, Allan.

DALE

O bliss!

MARGARET

Even before I married Harry I loved you. I could never make up my mind between the two of you. Finally I accepted Harry's proposal, not because I loved him more, but because . . . well, you were so shy, and it seemed you'd never get to the point.

DALE

I was so spellbound by your beauty I was powerless to let you know it.

MARGARET

And after I was married to Harry I could never quite make up my mind which of you I cared for most—Harry, the practical, cheerful, reassuring kind, or you—romantic, melancholy—the dreamer. I finally realized that I loved you both the same—that my heart was divided equally between you.

DALE

Equally?

MARGARET

Yes, equally. Even though I now confess my love for you, I can give you but half my heart. If Harry were to walk through that door at this moment, I would make the same admissions to him. My love for him has never abated either.

DALE

Then how—why did you marry Dexter?

MARGARET

I was so confused at the time. I had nowhere to turn, with my baby gone. He offered me security, protection—so I thought. Your red uniform seemed to remind me of Harry and the life I used to lead. I thought I might grow to care for him after our marriage. I was wrong!

DALE

That is all over now. Now we must plan how to get you out of his clutches.

MARGARET

Yes. There's not a moment to lose.

DALE

I think I have a scheme. Do you know that deserted cabin on the edge of town?

MARGARET

Yes.

DALE

You must go there—now—without letting anyone see you. I'll keep Dexter in conversation as long as I can—it will be some time before he discovers you're gone, and when he does he'll send for me and tell me to organize a search party. As soon as I can get free I'll come to you at the cabin—we'll set out this very night for Moose Junction!

MARGARET

But what then?

DALE

You can remain in the convent for a while. You'll be safe there, and you'll have plenty of time to decide.

MARGARET

Decide? Decide what?

DALE

Why, whether you want to marry me, of course.

MARGARET

Oh, Allan! You haven't even proposed!

DALE

I know, I'm slow about getting to the point. But I'm asking you now, Meg. Will you be my wife?

MARGARET

But I'm already married.

DALE

I haven't forgotten. But with my testimony and Mooka's you can easily get a divorce from Dexter. It's what you want, isn't it?

MARGARET

Allan dear, of course it is!

DALE

And . . . will you try to put Harry out of your mind?

MARGARET

I'll try, my dearest. I really will.

DALE

Then this is the happiest day of my life!

MARGARET

And of mine.

THE COMPROMISE

DALE

Now you must get a few things together—he mustn't come out and see us talking. Take the back way to the cabin—wear a hood, so no one sees your face. I'll be there as soon as I can.
(*Dexter enters.*)

DEXTER
(*glaring at them*)

Lieutenant! I was just coming to see what had happened to you. I presume Lucky Seven gave you my urgent message.

DALE

He did, Mr. Dexter. I was just inquiring of your wife where I could find you.

DEXTER
(*to Margaret*)

Leave us alone, please.

MARGARET

Yes, I think I will lie down. I had such a sleepless night.

DEXTER

Neither the Lieutenant nor I are interested in the state of your health. (*Margaret goes out.*) I mentioned that my message was urgent, Lieutenant. I'll get right to the point. Harry Reynolds is coming back to Cariboo.

DALE

Harry . . . coming back!

DEXTER

Yes. Does that surprise you so much?

DALE

Why, yes . . . er . . . He's been away so long.

DEXTER

You've turned pale, Lieutenant. Could it be that you have some reason for not wanting him to come back?

DALE

It's no pleasure to arrest an old friend, Mr. Dexter, even if he has turned out bad.

DEXTER

Is that all, Mr. Dale? Are you sure there isn't some other reason—some more personal reason—why you'd rather not see him?

DALE

What are you driving at?

DEXTER

I'm not given to eavesdropping, but I'm afraid that, quite by accident, I overheard the last part of your little love scene with my wife. A first-rate performance. I confess I was deeply moved.

DALE

You . . . you are ruthless!

DEXTER

Don't be angry with me. I mean it when I say I was moved by your performance. Such freshness, such poignancy. What was it she said? "My heart is divided equally between you."

DALE

You beast!

DEXTER

Careful, Lieutenant. Remember that it is *I* who am the injured party. I could have your badge, if I chose to. It wouldn't look very nice in the papers—"Mountie Tries to Abduct Young Wife from Home." For this reason, I urge you to cancel your projected trip to Moose Junction. In fact, I have taken steps to see that Margaret does not undertake this trip. My men are watching both doors of this cabin to prevent her.

DALE

You can't get away with this! No judge could fail to grant her a divorce after what she's told me about you.

DEXTER

I agree with you! And what's more, I'm going to give her complete freedom to act as she pleases. If she still wants to marry you, I'll do everything I can to enable her to. You see, I am capable of human feelings.

DALE

What do you mean, if she *still* loves me? Didn't she just say she did?

DEXTER

Yes—with half her heart. And you seem to forget the claimant of the other half is on his way here. That does change things, doesn't it?

DALE

What do you want of me?

DEXTER

Only this—when Reynolds walks in that door, I want you to shoot to kill.

DALE

Kill him? Harry? My oldest friend?

DEXTER

You'd be within your rights as an officer of the law—besides, I'd swear you did it in self-defense.

DALE

I couldn't think of it. It is my duty to arrest Harry, and then see that he is given a fair trial by jury.

DEXTER

Think, Dale. Your whole life is in his hands. Once Margaret knows he's still alive, that he still loves her, she'll fly to his side and you'll be forgotten. You forget they were once man and wife. Even if you send him to jail she'll wait for him—you don't know what perseverance that girl has.

DALE

It's impossible. But why are you so interested in getting rid of Harry?

DEXTER

Never mind that—just do as I say, if you value your happiness.

DALE

My happiness! Was it only a moment ago she said, "I love you?" It seems like a thousand years.

DEXTER

Follow my advice and all will be well.

DALE

I can't do it . . . or can I?
(*The door opens and Lucky Seven sticks his head in the room.*)

LUCKY SEVEN

We've spotted him. He head for this house—should be here in two minutes. Him wearum Indian outfit for disguise.

DEXTER

Excellent! You watch the back door and make sure she doesn't get out. We'll wait in here.

LUCKY SEVEN

Ugh!
(*He goes out.*)

THE COMPROMISE

DEXTER

Now listen, Dale. We'll hide behind this screen. When Reynolds comes in we'll take our time. Let him talk to her if he wants to—it will put him off his guard. When I give the signal, I want you to run out and challenge him in the name of the law. He'll reach for a gun of course, and then you'll fire the fatal bullet. Meanwhile I'll stand to one side and divert his attention so he doesn't get the draw on you—he's a superb marksman. Do you understand?

DALE
(*gloomily*)

Yes . . . I understand.

DEXTER

Then come on.
(*They hide behind the screen. After a few moments there is a knock on the door. Mooka comes out of the kitchen to answer it.*)

HARRY
(*disguised as an Indian*)

Is lady of house in?

MOOKA

Whatever you sell, we no wantum any.

HARRY

Me no salesman. Me wantum see lady of house.

MOOKA

Her not home. Who am you?

HARRY

Me good friend of lady of house.

MOOKA

Me never see you before.

HARRY

You think so? Look closer.

MOOKA

Me have to go now. Goodbye . . .
(*She is about to close the door.*)

HARRY

Wait. Showum this to white missus and tell her I want to see her.
(*He shows her something in his hand.*)

MOOKA

Baby Jim's little rattle! Where you get that?

HARRY

Never mindum. Send missus here.
(*Margaret enters.*)

MARGARET

Who is it, Mooka?

MOOKA

An old Indian with a message for you, missus.

MARGARET

For me? What sort of message?

HARRY

This is my message.
(*He shows her the rattle.*)

MARGARET

My baby's rattle! Where did you get it?

HARRY

That's my business.

MARGARET

Who are you, anyway?

HARRY

Don't you recognize me?

MARGARET

Your voice is familiar, but . . .

HARRY

Well, never mind who I am, for the moment. I have a few things to say first.

MARGARET

Leave us, Mooka. (*Mooka goes out.*) Do you know where my baby is? How do you happen to have this rattle?

HARRY

I picked it up outside your cabin shortly after the baby was kidnapped, when I was investigating the crime.

MARGARET

You investigated it? Then where is he—my baby, I mean?

HARRY

I don't know that. I do know the man responsible for the kidnapping, however.
(*Behind the screen Dexter is urging Dale to shoot, but the latter insists on hearing the rest of the story.*)

MARGARET

Who? . . . Who?

HARRY

By a strange coincidence, he is the same man who murdered old Mr. Stevenson, several years ago. (*Violent struggles from Dexter, behind the screen. He is held back by Dale.*) By an even stranger coincidence, that man is also your husband, *Mrs. Samuel Dexter!*

MARGARET

Oh, my goodness!

HARRY
(*sarcastically*)

You seem shocked by the news!

MARGARET

Shocked—but not surprised. I always had a feeling he was at the bottom of both crimes, but I had no clues to go on.

HARRY

You suspected your own husband?

MARGARET

Husband? Yes, in name perhaps he is my husband. But I have always hated him, and at last I know the reason why.

HARRY

You hate him—your own husband!

MARGARET

That's right.

HARRY

Then why did you marry him?

MARGARET

I don't think this is any of your business, old man, and besides, we're losing precious minutes, minutes in which we might discover where my baby is now.

HARRY

Oh, Margaret!

MARGARET

That voice . . . I know that voice!

HARRY
(*pushing back his hood*)

Now do you recognize me?

MARGARET

Harry!

HARRY

My dearest!
(*They embrace.*)

MARGARET

But why did you keep your identity a secret at first?

HARRY

I'm afraid I came back to taunt you with your marriage to a criminal, before I arrested him. Can you forgive me?

MARGARET

Of course! But tell me, Harry, how were you able to trace him?

HARRY

I found the rattle lying near the cabin, and near that a fur cap I knew belonged to Lucky Seven. From then on it was a simple, though long, process to trace the kidnapper and connect him with the murder of Stevenson.

MARGARET

But you haven't found Baby Jim?

HARRY

Not yet, but I have a hunch the case will break soon.

MARGARET

My hero! If you knew how I've longed for you every day of your absence!

HARRY

Not a single day has passed that I haven't thought of you with love and ... remorse.

MARGARET

But that's all over now . . . that last thing you spoke of.

HARRY

Yes . . . it's all over.
(*He kisses her.*)

DEXTER
(*coming out from behind the screen, with Dale*)
That's enough! Frisk him, Dale!

DALE

Harry Reynolds, it is my sad but unavoidable duty to arrest you in the name of His Majesty, the King.

HARRY

On what charges?

DEXTER

You'll find out soon enough.

DALE

On charges of robbery and kidnapping your own son.

HARRY

But you're mistaken . . . The man you want is right here in this room!

DEXTER

I'll say he is!

DALE

Any information you have will come out at your trial. Now I must ask you to accompany me to headquarters.

HARRY

Never . . . not while the real criminal is still at large. (*whipping out a gun*) Drop that pistol, Dale!

DEXTER

What's the matter, Dale? Are you scared? Well, if you won't do your duty, I will!
(*He charges at Harry with a knife, Dale shoots Dexter, who falls. Margaret screams.*)

DEXTER
(*laughing*)

You shot the wrong man, Dale. (*He dies.*)

DALE

He's dead!
(*Lucky Seven has sneaked into the house and is about to stab Dale in the back. Mooka comes quietly out of the kitchen and hits him over the head with a frying pan, knocking him cold.*)

DALE

Nice work, Mooka.

MOOKA

It not work . . . It a pleasure!

DALE

Now, Harry, if you'll drop that gun.

HARRY

Certainly, Allan. But believe me, the man you want is lying there . . . dead!

DALE

A jury will have to decide that. I heard your explanation to Margaret, and I must say it sounds rather weak.

MARGARET

He's telling the truth, Allan, I know he is!

MOOKA

Me too!

DALE

But where is the proof?
(*There is a knock at the door. Mooka answers it. The Chief, Daisy, Running Deer, Mountain Lion, Blue Feather, and other Indians come in.*)

CHIEF

We come from far to greet old friends!

RUNNING DEER

We very glad

MOUNTAIN LION

to be here! Ugh!

DAISY

Hi, everybody!

HARRY

Chief! Daisy! Running Deer! Mountain Lion! What are you doing here?

DAISY

We were just passing by and saw the smoke coming out of your chimney, so—

CHIEF

We bring pleasant news to white missus!

MARGARET

To me?

CHIEF

Yes—to you. But first, cannot these unpleasant sights be removed?
(*He gestures toward Dexter and Lucky Seven.*)

DALE

Give me a hand, boys. We'll lock up Lucky Seven and get Dexter out of the way too.
(*Dale and Mountain Lion carry Dexter off; Harry and Running Deer remove Lucky Seven.*)

THE COMPROMISE

CHIEF

And now, gather round. Me have little story to tell. Five years ago, one starless winter night, a baby was stolen from a cabin near here. As a dog sled whizzed over the trail from Cariboo to Elk City, a tiny immigrant rode in the observation car. This sled was being driven by an unscrupulous Indian, yet not one so unscrupulous that he preferred blood to money. Nearing our settlement, he met up with an old friend with whom he arranged a curious deal. But maybe, Blue Feather, you would like to take over the story from here.

BLUE FEATHER

Me ashamed, but me try. When Lucky Seven, for that name of Indian, see me he tell me have white baby he have to get rid of. Me remember prophecy, that white baby born to woman of our tribe restore us to prosperity. Accordingly, me take baby and make wife swear it hers.

CHIEF

Soon, prosperity return to Tobi tribe. Under the expert guidance of my new bride, my sons Mountain Lion and Running Deer, and, last but not least, myself, we build up rich fur-trading business.

DAISY

Now all the wigwams have indoor plumbing.

RUNNING DEER

Me drive team of eight dogs instead of four.

MOUNTAIN LION

Me buy ukulele and take lessons.

CHIEF

But me always remember prosperity founded on a trick. For me recognize Baby Jim when Blue Feather bring him in. And yet, me not able to bear disappointment of tribe. So me make up for it by giving Baby Jim every advantage of education and religious training. Can you forgivum me?

MARGARET

Of course we can!

HARRY

Yes, you may be sure of that.

MARGARET

But where is my baby? I'd like to see him.

CHIEF

And so you shall.
(*He claps his hands three times and Jim, now a boy of six, comes running in.*)

JIM
(*to Chief and Daisy*)

Daddy! Mommy! (*The Chief and Daisy embrace him fondly*) But where are the real Daddy and Mommy you said I'd meet?

MARGARET

Here I am, dear.

HARRY

I'm your real Daddy, son.

JIM

I'm pleased to know you.

MARGARET

If you knew how glad we are to have you back with us!

JIM

I'm pleased to know you, but these are my first Mommy and Daddy!

MARGARET

What!

DAISY

We've tried to reason with him, Mrs. Dexter, but he insists. He wouldn't even come with us until we promised to take him back.

THE COMPROMISE

CHIEF

He say he want to stay with us and study our religion.

JIM

Please, Mommy, it's what I really want. I'll always come and visit you.

MARGARET

Well, if your father thinks . . .

HARRY

I can see it's what he really wants. Jim, you may stay with the Chief, but once a year you must come and visit us.

JIM

I promise! Oh, thank you. Now I can study the ways of the raven god and try to be just like him!
(*Margaret dabs at her eyes with a handkerchief as Harry supports her.*)

MARGARET

Well, that's settled. But what is to become of us?

HARRY

Why we'll remarry, of course, and have other children, and Jim will be their big brother.

MARGARET

How devious fate is. Who would have thought this morning that so much joy would come to take place of sorrow!

INDIANS

Yes, the ways of the god are indeed inscrutable at first, though they are always plain in the end.

MARGARET

He leads us along dark paths, but eventually the light comes.

HARRY

Yes—underneath is always the primordial pattern.

DALE

Happiness for some—pain and suffering for others!

INDIANS

Who is this young man? His face seems pale and drawn with grief.

MARGARET

Alas! I gave him my heart, and now he thinks I want it back.

HARRY

You gave him—your heart?

MARGARET

Yes. Try to understand—I love you, but not you alone.

INDIANS

She loves the pale young man too!

CHIEF

Stranger things have happened.

DAISY

Yes—a heck of a lot stranger!

JIM

What is it? Why does everybody look so sad?

DAISY

You'll learn that in time, my son.

INDIANS

Oh great Spirit! See what a pass you have brought us to!

DALE

Why is joy always mixed with sorrow? Never have I tasted the pure essence of the former.

HARRY

She loves us both! Can this be?

MARGARET

Woe is me! What will become of us now? If only I could die—that would solve everything and the play could end. (*The author of the play enters.*) Who are you?

AUTHOR

The author of this play—the creator to whom you owe your very existence.

MARGARET

Have you come to help us out of this dilemma?

AUTHOR

I wish I could. Whenever I tried to imagine this play I could always get just this far and no further. Whom will you marry, I kept asking myself—the man of action or the melancholy dreamer? But even as I pondered the question I knew it made no difference, for you creatures are but the mere phantoms of my brain—shadows without substance!

In despair at not being able to think up an ending, I tried to emphasize other parts of the work. At least, the language will be perfect, I said, for I will make a study of human speech patterns and try to reproduce them exactly. But after months of study I could not find any patterns, so I had to give up the idea. I next tried to make my play sound elegant and poetical, hoping to please the critics, if not the audience. But my poetry, too, fell flatter than a bride's soufflé.

In despair I turned at last to the complex world of human relationships. Maybe, I thought, if I can't have anything interesting happen in the play I can at least show how people act when they are together, what their helloes are like and their goodbyes. But this attempt was a flop, too. I could find no rules or patterns for human behavior, and every action I observed seemed unlike every other action. It seemed there was nothing in life for my art to imitate!

By this time I had gotten on with the play by hook or crook, as you may have noticed. But I still needed an ending. What could I do?

And then I hit upon an idea which seemed brilliant to me and still does. My play would reflect the very uncertainty of life, where things are seldom carried through to a conclusion, let alone a satisfactory one. I would omit the final scene from my masterpiece! And you, vague and shadowy creatures, would not need any resolution of your imaginary difficulties, you could just walk off into the night, together . . . Where are you going? Stop!

(*A black scrim has fallen between the author, who is standing near the front of the stage, and the other players. They begin to retreat slowly backwards and the stage slowly gets darker. Margaret, spotlighted, flanked by Harry and Dale, smiles alternately at both of them, and both fondle her. Only the Chief, at the left of the stage in a spotlight, and Jim, who kneels before him, do not move.*)

MARGARET

It's been fun knowing you.

DALE

So long, old chap.

HARRY

Auf wiedersehen, and all that sort of thing.

AUTHOR

Don't! Where are you going? I haven't finished.

DAISY

But we have. It's time for us to go.

INDIANS

Farewell, old scout.

AUTHOR

You can't desert me! Not now! Chief, you stay behind at least, and Baby Jim!

JIM

Goodbye, Mr. Ashbery.

CHIEF

Now, spirit of the great raven, descend on your unhappy son. For of all of us, he suffers the most and knows the least.

AUTHOR

What are you doing to me? I'm beginning to feel funny.

CHIEF

Give him, for a while, the sleep you hold in your dusky sable plumes. And perhaps when he awakens the world and the people in it will be more the way he thinks they ought to be.

AUTHOR
(on his knees)

Hey, what the . . . Left all alone. Well, that's fine! Golly, I feel sleepy all of a sudden. What a nice comfortable stage this is. I think I'll just stretch out on it for a minute and catch a few winks. Maybe I'll have some pleasant dreams.

CHIEF

Sleep well, my son! Welcome, great brooding spirit of the night!
(*The spotlight on the chief goes off, and the stage is almost completely dark.*)

AUTHOR

Goodnight, everybody. Zzzzzzzz.
(*An actor dressed as an enormous raven walks on, picks up the author and carries him offstage.*)

CURTAIN

THE PHILOSOPHER

CHARACTERS

A masked man
Emily Maples, a middle-aged spinster
Carol, her seventeen-year-old niece
Napoleon ⎫
            ⎬ servants
Lily   ⎭
John Patterson, a reporter
Whitney Ambleside, a professor
  of oriental philosophy
Rocky Van Dusen, a prizefighter
Gloria Anderson, his girlfriend
Lawyer Flint
Tom Pembroke, ensign in the U.S. Navy
Count Sergei Oblomov
Soo Lin, a young Eurasian girl
Sheriff
A state trooper

The library at Woodlawn Hall, the Hudson River estate of the late millionaire eccentric, Jeremiah Maples. A huge, oak-paneled room in the Tudor style. At the left an enormous bay window with window-seat overlooking the Hudson, visible through the tops of the trees just underneath the window. At the right in the rear wall is a gothic arched door leading to the dining room—when it is open one can see the dining room table and chairs. To the left of this door is a large Renaissance fireplace—over it hang a shield and battle-axes. In the center of the back wall, a door leading to the hall. Another door in the right wall leads to the kitchen. Much of the wall space is taken up by bookcases—a gallery, with more bookshelves above it, runs around the room and is accessible by a flight of steps at far left. There are many signs of the late millionaire's fabulous art collections—old paintings, armor, oriental sculpture, and a large mummy case between the center door and the fireplace.

At the beginning of the play the room is dark. There are shutters over the windows. The furniture is draped in sheets and there are cobwebs everywhere, indicating that the house has been shut up for a long time. The time is late afternoon on Christmas eve in the early 1930's.

As the curtain rises a masked figure enters from the door at right and moves cautiously across the stage toward the windows. He opens one of the shutters and a beam of light enters the room. At that moment there is a sound of the big front door being opened, then closed, and voices and footsteps gradually approach the door at the center. The masked man hastily retreats from the window, and, not knowing where to hide, opens the door of the mummy case and steps inside, closing the door after him. The center door opens, and Emily, Carol, Lily and Napoleon enter—the latter weighted down with suitcases and an untrimmed Christmas tree.

CAROL

Gosh! What a spooky old place!

LILY

You said it!

NAPOLEON

Looks like King Tut's tomb to me.

EMILY

It certainly does, Napoleon. But when we get it tidied up a bit, with the tree trimmed and a roaring fire in the grate, it'll start looking more homey. The old place certainly has changed though. I can remember as a child coming to visit Uncle Jeremiah here, and playing dolls in that big bay window over there. That was before he became so eccentric and shut himself up here alone, with his millions and his oriental art collection.

CAROL

I just can't believe it, Aunt Emily. Only yesterday I was a naive little small-town girl, who'd spent all of her life—or as much of it as I can remember—in the bustling metropolis of Ashburton Falls, Massachusetts—population $746\frac{1}{2}$.

NAPOLEON

The half, that's me—Napoleon Z. Jones—on account of ah's only got half a brain.

LILY

That is the first intelligent remark you ever made.

CAROL

Nonsense, Lily, I only wish most folks had as many brains as Napoleon does. Anyway, here I am—spending Christmas eve in an old castle on the Hudson River. And on top of that I've seen Boston and New York, and driven in a taxi over the George Washington Bridge!

EMILY

And you'll be seeing lots more places, Carol honey, and going to college too, provided old Uncle Jeremiah remembered us in his will.

CAROL

Do you think he did?

EMILY

I don't know, dear. All I know is that three days ago, just one year after Jeremiah's death, Lawyer Flint sent me a telegram saying that according to the terms of Uncle's will, everyone whose name appears in it must spend Christmas eve here in Woodlawn Hall, where the will is to be read tonight after dinner.

LILY

Lawyer Flint axed you to get here early with your niece and two trusted family retainuhs, me and Napoleon, so as to get the place tidied up and the tree trimmed before the others arrive.

CAROL

If Great-Uncle Jeremiah asked specially for us to come and re-open the house, that must mean he left us something in the will!

EMILY

We mustn't count on it, Carol dear. Your uncle was as eccentric as they come—

LILY

Nutty as a fruit cake!

EMILY

Lily and Napoleon should know—they were his servants for years before his death. Since then, they've come to live with us in Ashburton Falls, even though their wages haven't always been too regular. . . .

NAPOLEON

Shucks, Miz Emily, we wouldn't leave you even if you wuz to pay us!

LILY

Sho' nuff!

EMILY

At any rate, Carol, I wouldn't get my hopes up for the will if I were you. Uncle Jeremiah never could forgive your poor mother, my sister, for eloping and running off to Hong Kong with that no-good speculator....

CAROL

They say she died of a broken heart, shortly after giving birth to me, in Hong Kong....

EMILY

Your father, like the hard-hearted chiseler he was, entrusted you to an American couple he scarcely knew, who were returning to the states.

CAROL

Luckily the couple were honest, and brought me straight to your door, Aunt Emily.

EMILY

I was able to identify you thanks to a note your dying mother had put into a little locket hanging around your neck, entrusting you to my care.

CAROL

On the same chain with the locket was this funny black stone with peculiar markings on it, which I've worn ever since. I imagine it's some trinket my mother bought in a bazaar in Hong Kong. Poor dear—it's probably the only thing she had to give me.
(*They all gather round Carol to look at the stone. At the same time the door of the mummy case slowly opens and then shuts again.*)

NAPOLEON

Do you feel a cold draught?

LILY

Yeah—and that reminds me—did you hear a funny noise as we were approaching the door of this room—sort of like footsteps?

EMILY

Come to think of it, I did. And look—that shutter is open. That seems awfully peculiar.

NAPOLEON

(*examining shutter*)

And they's fresh finger marks, heah in the dust on the shuttah!

EMILY

Maybe I'd better take a look around and make sure everything's in order.

NAPOLEON

Yeah—maybe *you* should.

EMILY

(*laughing*)

Now see here, Napoleon and everybody, let's not let the spooky atmosphere of this place get on our nerves. We have more important things to do. Lily, you go on out to the kitchen and get dinner started.

LILY

Yas'm, Miz Emily.

EMILY

You, Napoleon, go down cellar and chop some wood for the fireplace.

NAPOLEON

Did you say—down cellah?

EMILY

I didn't say the attic, silly. Here, take this if you're scared. (*She takes axe from over fireplace and gives it to him*). And don't come back without a big armload of wood!

NAPOLEON

Yas'm, I'll go—but it's unconstitutional, that's what it is!
(*He follows Lily off through the door at right.*)

EMILY

You can straighten up a bit in here, Carol. Open the blinds and take these moldy old sheets off the furniture. Brrr—they give me the creeps. I'll try and locate the Christmas tree ornaments. I believe they used to be in that big closet on the landing upstairs.

CAROL

How many guests are expected, Aunt Emily?

EMILY

There are five others, besides ourselves and Lawyer Flint. I suppose they're nieces and nephews from Aunt Sabrina's side of the family. They were always a queer lot—I never had much use for them. Still I guess we can't be too choosy tonight. I only hope it turns out to have been worth it—the trip here, and all.

CAROL

Don't think too much about that.

EMILY

I can't help it, dear. Besides you and me, there's Napoleon and Lily to worry about. With what I owe them in back wages, they could get married and have a home of their own. After all, they've been engaged now for seventeen years! (*The doorbell sounds.*) Good gracious, who can that be? The others weren't supposed to start arriving till around six, and it's barely four-thirty.

CAROL

Do you want me to go and see?

EMILY

No—I'll go. You fix up the place for our guests.
(*Exit through center door. Carol starts removing the sheets. She opens all the shutters.*)

CAROL

So that's the famous Hudson River! Sure makes the Ashburton River back home look like a creek. Wow! What a view! Pine-woods stretching all the way down to the shore. It's like some castle on the Rhine. Just the same, I'm glad I don't live here. There's something funny about this place. It's like—a feeling of death in the air.
(*During this speech the mummy case slowly opens—then shuts as Carol turns away from the window. Carol takes a feather duster and starts to dust bookshelves near window.*)
These books must have belonged to Great-Uncle Jeremiah. What weird titles—*Secrets of the Beyond*—he must know them all by now. *The Egyptian Book of the Dead.* This must explain all about mummies, like that one over there—how they were embalmed and then put into pyramids. (*She opens book.*) That's odd—here's a picture of a black stone with markings on it, just like the one around my neck. Let's see if I can make out what it says—the print is so fine. . . .
(*She takes book over to window. The masked man emerges from the mummy case and goes over to her, grabbing her from behind and attempting to remove chain with stone from around her neck. Carol screams and faints. The figure bends over her, trying to remove chain. At the sound of approaching footsteps, he grabs book and disappears through a secret panel in the bookcase. Just as he disappears, a piece of paper flutters out of the book to the floor near where Carol is lying. Enter Emily and John.*)

JOHN

Great Scott! What has happened here?

EMILY

Carol, honey! Speak to us! Oh, I never should have left her alone!

CAROL

Where am I? Wha-what happened?

EMILY

You're here with me, dear, at Uncle Jeremiah's place. (*She gets a decanter of brandy from a table.*) Here, drink this, dear. Oh—this is Mr. Patterson, a reporter from the *New York Times*.

JOHN

John Patterson. But let's save the introductions till later. First we must find out what happened to you just now. Why were you lying unconscious on the floor?

CAROL

I—I don't know. I was standing by the bookcase over there, when all of a sudden I heard a noise behind me. Before I could turn someone was clutching at me, trying to choke me.

EMILY

My poor baby!

JOHN

Did you get a look at the person?

CAROL

I tried to, but his face was covered by a mask. He kept pulling at this chain around my neck, as though he wanted to get this stone my mother gave me (*showing stone*). Then I must have fainted. (*She walks over to bookcase.*) That's strange—there's an empty place here in the bookcase. He must have taken the book I was reading—*The Egyptian Book of the Dead*.

JOHN
(*musingly*)

It *is* strange—stranger even than you think. Tell me . . . Carol, this stone with peculiar markings that you wear—you say your mother gave it to you?

THE PHILOSOPHER 131

CAROL

I think so, but I can't be sure. I never knew my mother, you see. I'm an orphan.

JOHN

Oh . . . I'm sorry.

EMILY

This is terrible! It may have been an escaped convict from Rockland County Penitentiary! Don't you think we'd better search the house at once, Mr. Patterson?

JOHN
(looking about)

No, whoever it was has had ample opportunity to give us the slip by now. This old place is probably full of secret rooms and passageways. I suggest we sit tight and wait for him to show himself again. Meanwhile Carol must not be left alone—obviously the criminal has a special interest in her.

EMILY

That's a good idea. You stay here with her, while I phone the sheriff to find out whether any convicts have escaped from the penitentiary.
(She goes out by the center door. The bookcase door flies open, and Napoleon stumbles into the room, dropping logs on the carpet.)

NAPOLEON

Did ah heah the word "penitentiary"? Ah only wish ah could escape *into* a nice wahm penitentiary. Ah's had jest about all ah can take of this crazy-house! Yas'm! Jest about enough!

CAROL

Napoleon! How did you get behind the bookcase?

NAPOLEON

Jest as ah finished choppin' wood, the candle ah took down cellah was blown out by a gust of wind. In the darkness I started walkin' up some steps, an' heah ah is! Funny thing—ah could've sworn ah heard somebody else movin' around down theah.

JOHN

It must have been the masked man who tried to strangle Carol.

NAPOLEON

Good gracious! Is yo' all right?

CAROL

Yes, but you'd better get out to the kitchen and make sure that Lily is. Mr. Patterson and I will build the fire. Here, Napoleon, take this along to be on the safe side (*handing him his axe*).

NAPOLEON

Tha'ss true. One old battleaxe deserves another. Hee, hee!
(*Exit.*)

JOHN

What a likable chap he is. Tell me, Carol, have you always been an orphan?
(*They begin to lay the fire.*)

CAROL

Mother died in Hong Kong when I was just a baby, and my father sent me back to America to be rid of me. I don't know whether he's still alive or not—and I don't much care, either. Aunt Emily is the only family I've ever known.

JOHN

Strange—I too am an orphan.

CAROL

That's a coincidence. Tell me, how does it happen that you're here for the reading of the will?

JOHN

As you may know, the Jeremiah Maples collection of oriental art is one of the finest in the western world. There have been rumors lately that the entire collection has been left to the Metropolitan Museum of Art, and the *New York Times* sent me here to find out if it was true. I also have another reason for wanting to be here, but I can't tell you what it is just yet.

CAROL

If Great-Uncle Jeremiah really left his collection to the museum, then that would mean it was a wonderful present to the whole population of New York City.

JOHN

That's right.

CAROL

I can't believe he would be that generous. From all I've heard, Jeremiah Maples was a mean old codger who detested his fellow man.

JOHN

Then who do you think will inherit his fortune?

CAROL

That's what's so puzzling. I know it won't be me, because he hated my mother. People say he had a soft spot in his heart for Aunt Emily, but he hadn't seen her for years before he died. Even Napoleon and Lily, his servants, hardly ever saw him. He used to shut himself up in the big tower at the north end of the castle. No one was ever permitted inside it, but they say he had installed some kind of laboratory there, and used to perform experiments. Perhaps he was trying to discover the secrets of the ancient Egyptians.

JOHN

It's interesting—what you say. Tell me, where is Uncle Jeremiah buried?

CAROL

I believe in the Homeville cemetery, not far from here. The funeral services were held in the strictest privacy—not one of the family was present. Why do you ask?

JOHN

Oh—no reason. (*changing the tone*) Say—do you know I kind of like you?

CAROL

That's funny. I do too. I guess orphans must understand each other. (*Emily enters.*)

EMILY

The sheriff is coming right over. Just as I suspected—a notorious gunman escaped from the penitentiary just this afternoon. He's known as "The Professor." He's middle-aged, suave, and distinguished looking—speaks with an Oxford accent. But he's one of the ten worst public enemies in the country. To think he may be under this very roof at this moment! (*The doorbell rings.*) Oh, who can that be?

CAROL

Be careful, Aunt Emily!

EMILY

Don't worry, dear—it's probably the sheriff. Keep an eye on her, Mr. Patterson.
(*Exit.*)

JOHN

A courageous gal, your Aunt Emily.

CAROL

Oh, I'm not worried about the killer as long as she's around.

JOHN

Just in case of an emergency, you'd better take this.

CAROL
A gun! But I've never shot a gun in my life.

JOHN
Then it's time you learned. Quick, put it away—someone's coming. (*Enter Whitney and Emily.*)

WHITNEY
I was driving on a back road near here when my limousine got stuck in the snow. I saw a light through the trees and headed toward it. I must ask you all to excuse me . . . (*looking around*) But . . . isn't this the house of my old teacher and friend, Jeremiah Maples?

CAROL
You mean you knew my great-uncle?

WHITNEY
Intimately, my dear child. Then you are his niece? Let me look at you. (*looking through pince-nez*) Yes—I see you have the same firm, uncompromising Maples features—belied by something elusive and twinkling in the eyes. . . . But you speak in the past tense. . . . Can it be then that my poor friend. . . .

EMILY
I'm afraid so. Uncle passed on a year ago.

WHITNEY
(*bowing his head*)

How dreadful! . . . I didn't know, you see. I only recently returned from a voyage of several years in the Orient. Allow me to present myself: Whitney Ambleside, professor of oriental philosophy at the Sorbonne in Paris.

CAROL
This is Mr. Patterson, a reporter.

WHITNEY
(*suspiciously*)

Indeed?

JOHN

Yes. Do you have any objections?

WHITNEY

With all due respect to you, my good man, I must say that the fourth estate has always filled me with a feeling akin to revulsion. A malicious rabble, seeking out all that is true and noble and secret in the human heart, and deliberately presenting it in a false and disgusting light.

EMILY

But Mr. Patterson is with the *New York Times*—in the archaeology department.

WHITNEY

In that case, Sir, I must offer you my apologies. You are—eh—engaged in bringing the light of the ancient world to our present dark ages—a noble endeavor, provided one is careful not to burn one's hands.

JOHN

What do you mean?

WHITNEY

Only that if the Ancients had their secrets, they intended them to remain secret. Knowledge is the property of the chosen few. Today we have another idea—that it should benefit the masses. Democracy, we call it. But who knows? Perhaps the only way we can benefit them is by keeping certain things hushed up.

EMILY

That's true—not everyone is an Einstein, after all.

JOHN

Thank goodness!

WHITNEY

In any case, young man, I apologize for my outburst. Obviously there is no connection between you and the vulgar muckrakers to whom I alluded.

JOHN

Not at all. But we'd better be going if you want me to push your car. The snow seems to be coming down faster.

WHITNEY

I'm afraid the case is quite hopeless, my dear fellow. What I'd hoped for was to telephone for a taxi to take me to the nearest village. I daresay there's a hotel near by where I can find a night's lodging.

EMILY

But of course we wouldn't dream of turning you out into the darkness and the snow. You'll stay here with us.

WHITNEY

You are too good to an old man. . . .

CAROL

Besides, if you were a friend of Great-Uncle Jeremiah's you may be mentioned in the will. . . .

WHITNEY

Will? . . .
(*The doorbell rings.*)

EMILY

That must be one of the heirs now! I'll explain it all to you later. You youngsters keep Professor Ambleside company while I answer the door. (*Exit.*)

WHITNEY

Nonsense, they don't need to bother about an old curmudgeon like me.

I'll just take my place in the chimney corner. H'm, what an interesting piece.
(*Takes object from mantel and examines it through magnifying glass. John takes Carol aside.*)

JOHN

Carol, I don't like that man's looks. I think your Aunt Emily was wrong to invite him to stay here.

CAROL

Nonsense, John. You're just angry because of his slighting remarks about journalists. Why he's a charming person—so cultured and distingué. I think Aunt Emily has a crush on him already.

JOHN

His description tallies exactly with that of the killer who just escaped from the penitentiary.

CAROL

Now you are being absurd. Just one look at Professor Ambleside should convince you he's incapable of evil.

JOHN

Just the same, I'm going to telephone the sheriff. This is too much of a coincidence.

CAROL

Are you insane? You'll just get an innocent man into trouble.

JOHN

It's you I'm trying to protect. I'll leave the door open while I'm in the next room. Don't hesitate to use the gun if he tries to pull a fast one.

CAROL

Oh all right. But I think you're being silly. (*Exit John. She approaches Whitney.*) Have you found something interesting?

WHITNEY

Curious, isn't it, my dear, that a humble artisan of 2,000 years ago could outsmart modern man and all his wonderful inventions? This tiny statuette from Asia Minor could not possibly be reproduced today.

CAROL

Really?

WHITNEY

Oh, a copy could be made, no doubt. But the soul would be lacking. Only centuries-old traditions and the loving touch of the craftsman can bequeath that to a work of art.

CAROL

I wish I knew more about the Ancients.

WHITNEY

There's no reason why you shouldn't, my dear. I should be glad to teach you. On condition that we don't infringe on the sacred mysteries I spoke of earlier.

CAROL

Oh, I wouldn't want to know them.

WHITNEY

On the other hand, a young, beautiful virgin like yourself might be the perfect receptacle for such secret lore. Tell me, my dear, has your heart remained pure? I mean, have you ever experienced love for anyone, other than your Aunt Emily of course.

CAROL

It's funny you should ask me that. Yesterday I'd have said no—but today I'm not so sure any more.

WHITNEY

Meaning?

CAROL

I think I'm getting to like that young reporter an awful lot. He's an orphan like me.

WHITNEY

I see. (*aside*) Curses—I'll have to work faster than I'd planned. (*aloud*) Well, before leaving I shall lend you a book which I'm sure will interest you.
(*Enter Emily, Rocky, Gloria; then John from right.*)

ROCKY

Hiya folks! Put her there, Unk! (*wringing Whitney's hand and whistling at Carol*) Some chick! Too bad I just got engaged.

GLORIA

Yeah, well don't forget it, ya punch-drunk punk!

WHITNEY

Who is this crude individual?

ROCKY

Sorry, Major Hoople. I always forgets me own strength. I'm Rocky Van Dusen, better known as the Tenth Street Tiger, Greenwich Village's gift to prizefighting. This broad is Gloria Anderson, my fiancée, well-known star of stage, screen, and burlesque.

GLORIA

We're both distant cousins of Aunt Sabrina, Uncle Jeremiah's late wife.

EMILY

Welcome to Woodlawn Hall. Have you known each other long?

ROCKY

Naw—we got engaged on the bus coming out here. The minute I saw her waitin' in line at the bus terminal I knew I'd seen her somewhere. Then she hitched up her stocking and I recognized her—Gloria "Goldilocks" Anderson—one of the most titillating temptresses of our time. A devotee of the terpsichorean art, I arranged to get the seat next to hers—and before we'd passed Sneden's Landing I was plightin' our troth with the ring I always carry for just such an emergency. (*Gloria shows ring.*) How do you like that, folks—a 21-carat zircon!

GLORIA

If anybody'd asked me this morning whether I believed in love at first sight, I'd have told him to go get his marbles examined. (*sighs*) I guess maybe the holiday season has something to do with it—plus this crazy business of the will. Tell me, are you folks all members of the family?

EMILY

No—just Carol and I are. Mr. John Patterson is a reporter from the *Times*, and Professor Ambleside is an old family friend whose car broke down near here.

ROCKY

Where did it break down?

WHITNEY

Er—on Highway 29, just south of Orangeburg.

ROCKY

That's funny—we passed through there on the bus and I didn't see nothin' of no broken-down car.

WHITNEY

Perhaps your powers of observation equal your superb command of English grammar. On the other hand it happened over an hour ago, and the snow has probably camouflaged it by now. Which reminds me that I'm feeling a bit exhausted by the long trek here in the cold—I wonder if you'd all excuse me if I retired for a short nap before dinner.

EMILY

Of course not—I'll show you to your room and have Napoleon bring you up a hot toddy. You shouldn't fatigue yourself that way.
(*They go out.*)

GLORIA

(*pointing to mummy case*)

Hey—he forgot his nightshirt.

ROCKY

Now that Gramps has gone, I'd like you kids to join me in a toast to my unblushing bride-to-be. I see Uncle Jeremiah was thoughtful enough to leave us a bottle of his best booze at least. (*They toast Gloria.*) Here's to love at first sight and the shapeliest gams that ever trod the boards of Minsky's.

JOHN

I'll second that—especially the first part of the sentence.

ROCKY

Gee—this stuff is potent. Too bad we killed the bottle. I wonder where the old goat used to hide the stuff.

JOHN

They say he had a laboratory in the tower at the north end of the house—maybe there's a still there.

ROCKY

That's an idea. I think I'll just mosey up and have a look-see.

GLORIA

Rocky! Remember you're in training.

ROCKY

Don't worry, toots. We'll practice my wrestling technique as soon as I get back—with the hooch.
(*Exit.*)

GLORIA

That's what he thinks. Well, I ain't complaining so long as he *gets* back. Frankly this place is beginning to give me the heebie-jeebies. I think we should all stick together for mutual protection. This whole business about coming out here to hear the will read sounds fishy to me. I never even heard of Uncle Jeremiah until I got Lawyer Flint's letter yesterday.

JOHN

Gloria's right. Why, just before you got here Carol was attacked by a mysterious masked stranger. He may be one of us, for all we know.

CAROL

Then we should make sure that there are always at least three of us together at one time. (*The doorbell rings.*) Oh—there's the doorbell. Aunt Emily's upstairs with the professor—I'd better go.

JOHN

Be careful. Don't hesitate to defend yourself first and ask questions afterward. (*Exit Carol.*) Well, that leaves two of us alone. I hope you're not scared.

GLORIA

More chilled to the bone than scared. I wish Rocky would get back with that firewater. (*The lights go off.*) What the—

JOHN

The lights have gone off! Here, Gloria, take this axe just in case anything happens. I'm going to try to find the fuse box.

GLORIA

All right—but hurry. I may look like a cave-woman but I'm not too much of a hand with an axe. (*Exit John.*) All alone in the dark—with King Tut's mother-in-law. Well, girl, that's what you get for being mercenary. Oh, why did I come out here anyway, when I could be back at Minsky's walking down a nice warm runway. And when I

think they were about to promote me to more pay and less of a costume. 'Course I wouldn't have met Rocky if I hadn't come here. Oh, why doesn't that cauliflower-eared Casanova get back here! (*The lights come on.*) Whew! That's more like it. (*She has been pacing back and forth with the battle-axe and is now in front of the bookcase. She spies paper on the floor.*) What the heck's this? (*reads paper*) Hey, this looks serious! John! John! Where are you!
(*Masked figure steals out of bookcase and hits her over the head. Takes paper, reads it, and throws it into fireplace. Picks up Gloria and vanishes into bookcase as John enters.*)

JOHN

Yes, Gloria, what is it? Great Scott—she's vanished!
(*Sees paper in fireplace and picks it up, reads it, and thoughtfully pockets it.*)

CAROL
(*returning*)

That's funny—when I got to the door there was no one there. Where's Gloria?

JOHN

She—er—stepped out of the room for a moment to powder her nose. You say there was no one at the door?

CAROL

No—there weren't even any tracks in the snow. Whoever rang the bell must have done so from inside the house. But why? If it was the masked burglar, then why didn't he try to kidnap me again?

JOHN

We may be finding that out all too soon. Now, Carol, I want you to promise me one thing. Whatever may happen this evening, however strangely I may seem to be behaving, I want you to promise not to lose faith in me. Agreed?

THE PHILOSOPHER   145

                              CAROL
Of course, John. What a funny request!

                              JOHN
I knew I could trust you. Now I want to ask you one more favor. I want you to shut your eyes for a minute.

                              CAROL
Like this?

                              JOHN
That's right. Now stay that way just a minute.
(*He kisses her.*)

                              CAROL
John dear!

                              JOHN
Carol—
(*Aunt Emily and Whitney enter. Emily is too absorbed in what Whitney is saying to notice the embrace.*)

                              EMILY
And you say that the gem of your collection is a piece of onyx known as the Susa scarab? But just why is it so precious? I thought onyx was a semi-precious stone.

                              WHITNEY
It's worth, my dear Miss Maples, has nothing to do with its physical properties. Oh, I'll grant you the scarab is a lovely piece—a shimmering black stone exquisitely carved in the form of a beetle—the Egyptian symbol of life. Any museum would be glad to own it. And yet its true value is inestimable—and known only to me.

                              JOHN
Just what is so valuable about the stone, Professor Ambleside? Don't keep us all in suspense.

WHITNEY

(*looking mysterious*)

Normally it's a thing I prefer not to talk about. The ordinary run of human beings are apt to scoff and think me an old fogey ... but I see I have a sympathetic audience.

CAROL

We're dying to know the secret.

WHITNEY

Are you, my child? Very well, I'll tell it to you. But you must promise not to mention it to a soul outside this room. Indeed the consequences—both for yourselves and for me—would be most unfortunate were you to do so.

CAROL

Oh, we promise!

EMILY

Yes, of course we do.

JOHN

(*somewhat testily*)

Of course, of course. Now please get to the bottom of all this. Why all this mystery around a simple piece of stone in your scarab collection?

WHITNEY

(*glancing first at John*)

Because, my fine young friend, this simple stone as you call it is the clue to a secret that has puzzled mankind for centuries! The great secret! The only secret worth knowing! Next to my scarab the philosopher's stone itself is as a worthless pebble!

JOHN

What do you mean?

THE PHILOSOPHER

WHITNEY

Just this: in the days of the pharaohs, experiments were made to prolong human life. You have all seen the Egyptian mummies preserved in museums, and of which my dear late friend Jeremiah had such a superb collection (*indicating mummy case*). You know that the scientists of those days had discovered ways of preserving the human body which have now been forever lost in the confusing mists of time. But this was only part of their activity—the lesser part, I might add. For what good after all is the human body, no matter now lifelike it is, if the spark of life has gone?

JOHN

Just what are you getting at?

WHITNEY

Scientists today are fairly certain that the Egyptians had discovered a way of prolonging that spark—of keeping it glowing for hundreds, even thousands of years—perhaps for all eternity. It is even rumored that some men walking the earth today first saw the light of day beside the sluggish waters of the Nile, centuries upon centuries ago.

JOHN

But that's . . . that's impossible!

WHITNEY

Do you find it so? At any rate this aspect of the thing is not my main concern. I am only a humble archaeologist, not a biologist. What interests me is the historical importance of the discovery—its importance in the history of ideas of immortality. Viewed in this light, my scarab is of immense importance, for it contains the secret formula for immortality discovered by the ancient Egyptians.

CAROL

Gosh!

JOHN

Has anyone ever tried putting the formula to the test?

WHITNEY

Unfortunately, it's not quite that simple. The formula itself is written in a secret language, of which all trace has vanished. I myself have spent half a lifetime trying to decode it—in vain.

EMILY

Then how do you know that what's written on the stone *is* the secret of eternal life?

WHITNEY

Because the inscription on the other side of the scarab—in ordinary hieroglyphics—says so. And I have every reason to believe it's true. It also speaks of the existence of another scarab, similar to the one I own, which contains the key to the secret language in which the formula is written. I needn't bother to tell you that this second scarab has been the object of a lifelong search on my part.

JOHN

How do you know the scarab still exists? How do you know it hasn't been lost somewhere—in the mists of time, as you say?

WHITNEY

According to the inscription in hieroglyphics, this cannot happen. The missing scarab protects itself and the person who wears it. It can belong only to someone who is pure in heart. Of course the person who owns it has no idea of what it is or its magic powers. At the end of his life, however, he automatically passes it on to another person, pure in heart like himself, though he has no idea of why he is doing so. In this way the scarab (if we are to believe the inscription) has been handed down from generation to generation ever since ancient times.

JOHN

Sounds pretty far-fetched to me.

WHITNEY

Perhaps so. In any case, I should like to find the missing scarab, decode the message, and judge for myself. Unfortunately I have exhausted the better part of a lifetime and a large personal fortune trying to do so. My resources as well as my energies are almost at an end.

EMILY

Can't you interest some wealthy person in the cause, and get him to invest some money?

WHITNEY

Alas, no. I have long since given up trying to interest people—everyone thinks I'm slightly potty when I mention this quest that has sapped all my forces. Even your uncle Jeremiah was inclined to take a skeptical attitude.

JOHN

And you came here tonight hoping to find Uncle Jeremiah and persuade him to change his mind.

EMILY

Oh, stop badgering the professor, John. He already told us his car broke down while he was driving near here . . . (*to Whitney*) It certainly sounds like a worthy cause all right. Perhaps you'll be finding backers for your project sooner than you realize. Depending on what happens here tonight, of course.
(*Rocky enters.*)

ROCKY

Hey, get a load of this, folks! (*brandishing bottle*) Genuine twelve-year-old scotch, aged in the wood. And you know where I found it? In Uncle Jeremiah's laboratory! I guess the old bat wasn't as cracked as we figured! (*He uncorks a bottle and pours himself a glass.*) A toast to you all, on the eve of this gala family reunion—you too, Uncle Jerry, if you can hear me! I hope what they serve you up there is as good as what you left behind!

WHITNEY

(knocking glass out of his hand)

Drop that glass, you bubble-brain! Don't you realize that stuff is a deadly poison, unless taken in infinitesimal quantities?

ROCKY

Now look, Pop, I don't know what stuff *you've* been takin', but have a care. . . . Nobody deprives Rocky Van Dusen of his libation with impunity.

JOHN

Just what makes you so sure of yourself, Professor? After all the bottle is clearly labelled Scotch.

WHITNEY

I . . . er . . . Well, you see Jeremiah's laboratory technique was always a bit helter-skelter and . . .

ROCKY

And you wanted to keep all the sauce for yourself. Yeah, I see. How do you like that, honeybunch . . . Hey, Gloria—where did she go, anyway?

JOHN

Oh, I forgot to tell you. While you were upstairs she received an urgent phone call and left immediately for New York. She left word for you to call her as soon as you get back.

EMILY

That's strange—I didn't hear the phone ring.

CAROL

I didn't either. Why didn't you mention this before, John? You told me Gloria had stepped out of the room to powder her nose.

JOHN

Well, she did say something about sprucing up a bit before she went back.

ROCKY

Hey, wait a minute—there's someting fishy about all of this. She was in such a hurry to get back she couldn't wait for me, but she found time to powder her proboscis? You ain't bein' square with me, friend.

JOHN

I've told you all I know. . . . At least, I'm not at liberty at present to reveal anything that might . . .

ROCKY

Yeah, what about that, huh? You better start revealin' now and fast, unless you want Santa Claus to find you hangin' on the mantelpiece next to your stockin'.

CAROL

John, if you know some secret information about Gloria's disappearance, please tell it!

JOHN

I can't say anything more—all I know is that she received a phone call, and right after that she called a taxi and left.
(*The doorbell rings.*)

EMILY

That must be Gloria now—the snow was probably too deep for the taxi to get through.

CAROL
(*going to answer it*)

I'll get it, Aunt Em.

EMILY

Now aren't you boys sorry you let your nerves get the better of you. Shame on you both.

ROCKY

I'll extend me apologies after I've seen who comes in that door.
(*Enter Carol and Flint.*)

EMILY

Good heavens! Why, it's Lawyer Flint!

FLINT

And just what is so extraordinary about that? You *were* expecting me, weren't you?

EMILY

Yes, but—gracious, so many things have been happening all at once. I feel a little dizzy. . . .

FLINT

Well, perhaps someone else could explain why you're all staring at me as though I'd come back from the dead.

ROCKY

Foist, let me ask you a question. Did you see anybody driving away from here in a taxi as you came up to the house?

FLINT

Of course not. The drive was completely deserted—and no car could have gotten through anyway. The drifts are two feet deep in places.

ROCKY

OK, that settles your hash, Mr. Reporter. Since you won't tell *us* where Gloria is, maybe the cops can persuade you to talk. Keep an eye on him, folks, while I telephone—he's as slippery as they come.
(*Exit.*)

JOHN

This is absurd! I know nothing about Gloria's whereabouts.

EMILY

I believe you, John, and I think Carol does. But you were the last person to see her, and there are several contradictions in your story.

THE PHILOSOPHER

FLINT

Will someone please tell me what's going on? After all I am a person of some consequence here.

CAROL

I'll explain, Lawyer Flint. I'm Uncle Jeremiah's grand-niece, Carol. I had just gone to answer the doorbell when this young man....

FLINT

And what is his name, pray tell?

CAROL

John Patterson. He's a reporter from the *New York Times*.

FLINT

What! You mean you let a reporter in here?

CAROL

He's from the archaeology department. Anyway, no sooner had I left the room when the lights went out. (*They go out.*) ... It's happened again!

EMILY

Eek! I felt something cold brush my arm!

CAROL

I did too! Where are you, Aunt Emily?

EMILY

Over here, dear, near the fireplace.

FLINT

I felt something too! Will you please stop shoving me, whoever you are! (*The lights come on.*) Whew! I must be covered with bruises. Wha ... what's this! My briefcase with the will! It's gone! Someone took it!

ROCKY
(re-entering)

The bulls will be right over. They're anxious to have a look at this so-called reporter.

FLINT

And not a moment too soon! While you were out someone stole the will!

EMILY

It's too terrible!

ROCKY

Don't move, anybody. I think I have a pretty good idea where that will is. OK, you, raise your arms while I frisk you.

JOHN

Like fun, I will!

ROCKY

Oh, a wiseacre. OK, I'll knock you out first, if you want it that way. (*They scuffle.*)

EMILY

Boys, stop it! Let's talk this over calmly and—

WHITNEY

Disgusting!

CAROL

Can't you be reasonable, John?
(*John KO's Rocky.*)

JOHN

That'll teach you, you young hothead.

CAROL

You brute! You've knocked him out cold.

JOHN
I had to, Carol. It was in self-defense.

CAROL
Don't speak to me. I hate violence and brutality. Aunt Emily, is there any more of that *eau de vie*? I'll force some down his throat. You get some cold compresses.

JOHN
(pulling a gun)
See here, everybody, I'm sorry to do this, but maybe later you'll understand why.

EMILY
He's got a gun!

JOHN
Please keep calm. I should hate to be forced to use it, but if one of you should try to stop me—even you, Carol—I should be forced to act in your common interests.

CAROL
Monster!

FLINT
Don't goad him. He's already a desperate man.

JOHN
(backing towards door)
You're right, I am desperate—desperate to find out what happened to Gloria and to get to the bottom of this whole ugly mess. You've forced me to behave brutally. I only hope you may thank me later for what I—
(He backs into Tom Pembroke in the doorway who disarms him).

TOM
Rather a nasty-looking toy, young fellow. Santa Claus bring you that?

EMILY

Thank heavens!

WHITNEY

Be careful! That man is desperate.

TOM
(*holding John*)

Oh, I don't think he'll be causing anybody any more trouble. Allow me to present myself, folks—Tom Pembroke, Aunt Sabrina's great-nephew, and ensign in the United States Navy. I got my notification from Lawyer Flint only yesterday, and my leave came through this morning. I rushed up from Norfolk as fast as I could.

JOHN

By what train? The only train from Norfolk arrives two hours from now.

TOM

Now who gave you permission to talk? And who told you I took the train? As a matter of fact I took the bus.

JOHN

That's a lie—the bus from Norfolk doesn't arrive in New York until after midnight.

CAROL

Ignore him, Mr. Pembroke. We all can never be grateful enough to you for saving our lives.

JOHN

Carol, this man is a dangerous fake! Can't you see he's lying? He's no more a naval officer than I am.

WHITNEY

Allow me to join my voice to the general chorus of gratitude, sir. You have delivered us from the hands of a homicidal maniac.

TOM

All in the line of duty, sir.

FLINT

All this doesn't solve the problem of my missing briefcase with the will in it. If he took it while the lights were out, what did he do with it? Where is it?

NAPOLEON
(*entering with Sergei and Soo Lin*)

Heah's some moah calluhs says they's come fo' the readin' of the will. (*Doorbell rings.*) Well, I'll be switched—it nevuh rains but it pours, no suh! Aw, I'se comin', I'se comin'!

SERGEI
(*Russian accent*)

Excuse us, pliz. We seem to be intruding on a private conversation.

EMILY

Not at all. I'm Miss Maples, Uncle Jeremiah's niece. May I ask your names?

SERGEI

Of course—forgive me my oversight. Count Sergei Oblomov, the last of the Oblomovs (*kisses her hand*).

CAROL

A Russian count!

SERGEI

That is exact. My beloved wife, the late Countess Mamie Oblomov, was the niece of Aunt Sabrina, Uncle Jeremiah's wife.

EMILY

And who is this pretty creature?

SOO LIN

Me Soo Lin—Eurasian daughter of former Hong Kong housekeeper of Uncle Jeremiah. Me velly suplised to get notice of mention in will. Uncle Jeremiah always velly kind—but me last see him when only a little girl. Since then pellents die—me embark on tlamp steamer to see your beautiful countly where I get job in hand laundly on Mott Stleet.

CAROL

You're from Hong Kong! That almost makes us sisters—I was born there, you see.

SOO LIN

Soo Lin's one wish—to buy contlolling intelest in hand laundly and use plofits to take voyage to Hong Kong to see old home, old fliends. Maybe you come too.

FLINT

Nobody's going anywhere until that will is found. Where in tarnation are those stupid flatfoots?

NAPOLEON
(*opening door*)

Dey is heah!
(*Enter Sheriff and a state trooper.*)

SHERIFF

Don't nobody make a move. I've got you all covered.

FLINT

That is entirely unnecessary. It was we who summoned you here—to find a missing will and a missing girl.

WHITNEY

Gloria's disappearance was most unfortunate. But perhaps the will is our most immediate concern, since it vanished in this very room five minutes ago, and is no doubt still here.

JOHN

That's a ridiculous supposition! And meanwhile a girl's life may be at stake while you stand around quibbling over a piece of paper!

SHERIFF

Who is this young whippersnapper?

JOHN

Never mind who I am. Your business is to find Gloria, as long as you're here.

SHERIFF

Say, you ain't a-goin' to try to teach me my job, are you, young feller? At my age—

JOHN

Idiots!

WHITNEY

Obviously this is all a clumsy manoeuver to distract our attention from the missing will. But if this young man is really concerned about Gloria, there is an easy and efficacious way of putting his sincerity to the test. Let the two gentlemen of the law search everyone in the room to make sure one of us is not detaining the will. Having ascertained that the will is not among us, we then form a search party to look for Gloria. I shall be delighted to volunteer first to be "frisked" as I believe you call it. (*Steps forward with arms raised in the air.*)

JOHN

Not me! You won't get me that way, Ambleside!

EMILY

What does he mean?

CAROL

It's simple, Aunt Emily. If John were innocent he'd let the sheriff search him.

JOHN
Carol—how can you believe such a thing?

SHERIFF
All right, young'un. Reckon as how we better start with you. Raise your arms in the air. That's right.
(*John does so but brings oriental spear on wall down on heads of two policemen and Tom, knocking them off balance, and dashes through rear door. They start to rush after him but Napoleon appears in the door with a big gong which he strikes.*)

NAPOLEON
Dinnuh is served! (*Everybody but the unconscious Rocky rushes out after John.*) Well ah sweah, nevuh did ah see such a hungry bunch of free loaduhs! Such mannuhs! (*noticing Rocky*) Say, is yo' deaf or sumthin'? (*striking gong*) Second and last call for chow!

ROCKY
(*staggers up and starts to box Napoleon, then collapses on his shoulder*)
Hey, you can't count me out—I had one elbow off the floor! Lemme at him—I'll clobber the sonofagun!

NAPOLEON
(*pushing him back into chair disgustedly*)
Aw, get back in yo' cohnuh, John L. Sullivan! The fight ain't even begun yet!

CURTAIN